The Pocket
WILLIAM LAW

The Pocket

WILLIAM LAW

With a Foreword by the
ARCHBISHOP of YORK

Edited by
ARTHUR W. HOPKINSON

A threefold cord is not quickly broken.
—Ecclesiastes 4:12

Philadelphia
THE WESTMINSTER PRESS

First Published in Great Britain in 1950
by Latimer House Limited

Grateful acknowledgment is made to
Harper & Brothers for the quotations
on pages 9 and 10 from Henri Talon,
*William Law, A Study in Literary Crafts-
manship*, 1949.

FOREWORD

To THE majority of English Churchmen, William Law is known only for his *Serious Call*. Comparatively few know that he was the author of many other books, and still fewer have read anything except a few extracts from them. Mr. Hopkinson is here attempting to remedy this defect by making an abridgment of three of his lesser-known works. It is a bold step to abridge the writings of an author, and he who undertakes it lays himself open to the attacks of indignant critics. But abridgment is sometimes necessary if additional readers are to be secured; for many today hesitate at plunging into books which, at first sight, appear unnecessarily discursive and which are made formidable to the modern reader by an excessive use of capitals and italics. Mr. Hopkinson can, however, be trusted to undertake the work of abridgment with discretion and wisdom, for in a previous book he has shown that he is a devoted disciple of William Law. The reader can be assured that he has preserved carefully all that is best both in the matter and form of a writer who was not only a great master of the spiritual life, but also a master of the English language. The message of a man like Law, with his clear insight into human character and motive, and with his prophetic emphasis on the fundamental difference between right and wrong, is of special value in an age when moral distinctions are often blurred. This abridged edition should make Law's writings familiar to many who otherwise would be ignorant of them.

CYRIL EBOR.

INTRODUCTION

To record that William Law wrote *A Serious Call to a Devout and Holy Life* and that William Cowper wrote *John Gilpin* is not to pronounce the final word about Law as a religious writer or Cowper as a poet. But whereas *John Gilpin* discloses an unexpected aspect of the "Striken Deer" of Olney, the *Serious Call* is part and parcel of Law's characteristic writings. It would, however, be almost as unfair to speak of Law as if he had written nothing else as it would be to sum up Cowper as merely the author of *John Gilpin*.

That is the justification of this book—the desire to present William Law in his many-sidedness; and so let him speak for himself rather than through the agency of some commentator who is only interested in one side of his work. Not one person in a hundred of those who have read the *Serious Call* has read anything else that Law wrote. And, with the exception of various departmental "selections" from his writings, nothing else of his is available in print at the present time. It may be, though I doubt it, that the *Serious Call* is his greatest as well as his most popular book; and that, here, *vox populi* is *vox Dei*. Yet the fact remains that Law was far too great and many-sided a man to be judged by one book.

The *Serious Call* may account for his influence with the Evangelical Movement in the Church of England and the splendid moral stability underlying the work of the "Clapham Sect" But it does not account fully for the influence he had in shaping, to some degree, the course of the Catholic Revival in the Oxford Movement. Nor did it play the part that some of his other writings played

7

in preparing for the resurgence of Mysticism and the "religion of experience" which, under the stimulus of W. R. Inge, marked the beginning of the twentieth century.

Religion, the bond which joins man to God, is a rope of many strands. Neither Authority, nor Reason, nor Experience is enough, by itself, to make the bond complete. All three must contribute to its strength. It is the glory of William Law that, in his religious writings, he wove a threefold cord which is not quickly broken. Until the time, much to be desired, when the whole of his writings are reprinted and made available for those interested in the religious history of England during the last two hundred years, it seems worth while to re-issue three of his most characteristic works, dealing with the three main strands which go to make up true religion. It is not a full meal; but at any rate it is an appetizer.

The *Treatise on Christian Perfection*, though it has less popular appeal than the *Serious Call*, is a more complete work and less "dated" by references to transient social conditions. But it is long and the second part is cast in the form of a dialogue; a literary device in which Law most assuredly did not excel. So, in spite of leaving out many beautiful passages in Part II, only Part I is given here. I have chosen *The Spirit of Prayer* rather than *The Spirit of Love* to exhibit the mystical strand in Law's religion, because it seems to me more first-hand; there is more of Law and less of Behmen. The *Appeal* chooses itself; for it is unquestionably the best short account of that body of tradition and authority which Law recognized as an essential factor and guide in the life of a religious man. In chronological order the dates of the three books are that the *Treatise* was published about 1726, the *Appeal* about 1740 and *The Spirit of Prayer* nine years later, in 1749.

About William Law, apart from his writings, little need be said, and that little I have said already.[1] He was born

[1] *About William Law*, Arthur W. Hopkinson (S.P.C.K. 8s. 6d.).

in 1686, and died in 1761. As he could not conscientiously swear allegiance to the reigning monarch, he was debarred from any official standing in the ministry of the Church of England. He was a preacher without a pulpit, a priest without an altar. He was an ascetic, but his doting house-keepers seem to have enforced a considerable degree of comfort upon him. In any case, his asceticism took the form of a grim austerity rather than an exuberant Franciscan love of Lady Poverty. Gifted with a penetrating wit, he was, none the less, devoid of any sense of humour; for he was incapable of laughing at himself. He had many admiring disciples and a few devoted companions; but he had no friends, if a friend is one who knows your faults and loves you all the same. The traffic of friendship can only circulate on a two-way road. So, for many reasons, writing was Law's only outlet and means of self-expression. This had its advantages in that it enabled him to concentrate the whole force of his genius and his personality on his writing. But naturally there were disadvantages; for his environment was not stimulating and he had little oppor-tunity of rubbing up against intellects on a par with his own. This had the inevitable result of deepening his besetting failing, the tendency to become pontifical. The man who thinks himself *always* right is never entirely persuasive.

He lives in his writings—the outward course and events of his life are of little importance. It is fortunate, therefore, that with the present revival of interest in eighteenth-century literature, there has appeared a book (in 1948) which, to an extent not attempted before, deals with him as a master of literature.[1] It is the work of a learned Frenchman whose understanding of Law and whose com-mand of pure English put most Englishmen to shame, while it earns the gratitude of all lovers of Law. Though

[1] *William Law, A Study in Literary Craftsmanship*, Henri Talon (Rockliff 8s. 6d.).

described as *A Study in Literary Craftsmanship*, it is something
much more and throws a new light on many of the problems
which students of Law have to face. The author, Dr.
Talon, not only claims for Law that he is a literary crafts-
man of whom it may be said that "the value of his style
lies in its accuracy, in its close adherence to his ideas,
which is precisely the supreme criterion of good prose"[1]
but he also maintains that high as is the standard of the
controversial and ethical books, there is still a gradual
progression in his perfecting of his style, which finds its
climax in some of the mystical books of his later period:
"Finally, the weather in the heart of the mystic brings
about a blooming of his style. Whereas formerly it lacked
colour, it has now a few bright tints and, more generally,
soft, subdued tones, like a painting mellowed by time.
Above all, it is more musical and really seems to catch the
harmonies of the spirit."[2] With this judgment I cannot
agree. Law's earlier writings seem to me to have a con-
ciseness and a clarity which are less noticeable in the more
elaborate outpourings of his later period, when, in spite
of many passages of outstanding beauty, there is something
rather ponderous about his Behmenism. But this is simply
a matter of differing taste. Dr. Talon does not disparage
the earlier writings; I do not disparage the later. We are
happily agreed that to William Law should be accorded
a front place and a high fame among English men of letters.

As regards the *form* in which this edition of Law's three
books is presented: a friend wrote to me that he would
like to read more of William Law, but he found himself
"choked by his capitals". The complaint is just, for Law,
like many of his contemporaries, was lavish in his use of
capital letters. They sprout on his pages like bristles on
the face of a man who has lost his razor. To shave them off
is not to disfigure Law, it makes him more presentable to
modern readers who are used to a more restrained use of

[1] Op. cit. p. 15.   [2] Op. cit. p. 61.

capitals. It also seems better to leave in ordinary type a good many words and phrases that Law puts into italics. The reviewer who described Hilaire Belloc's *History of the First World War* as "marred by the italicization of the obvious" was expressing a criticism which applies to any unnecessary use of an artificial emphasis in literature. So there has been a pruning of italics in this reprint.

Thirdly, there is the matter of punctuation: every writer seems to have his own usage and it would be a bold man who claimed that in English literature there were precise and unalterable rules of punctuation. But Law defies all reason and custom in his use of stops. He sprinkles them over his pages like a cook shaking out flour from a dredger and with far less discrimination. The changes in punctuation, which I have ventured to make, are probably far from perfect; but they are meant to contribute towards easier reading and understanding.

I have felt little hesitation about the desirability of bringing the original use of capitals and italics and the punctuation in these writings into closer conformity with modern usage, because anything that makes an author more easily readable, without altering his meaning and purpose, is justifiable. When it comes to the question of abridging the three books here reprinted, I am in a fix; for it is always difficult to justify abridgment and still more difficult to abridge fairly. But, in order to include in one volume of reasonable size these three most characteristic specimens of Law's teaching, it is necessary to attempt the thankless and unwelcome task of abbreviation. In doing this, it became clear that there is not so much loss in an abridgment of William Law as there would be in the case of an author less discursive and diffusive. Even Dr. Talon mentions "the calculated monotony" in the pattern of successive sentences; though he asserts, rightly, that Law is "never redundant through carelessness". There are, moreover, occasional passages which had only a temporary importance; as, for instance, in the *Treatise on Christian Perfection,* the many pages of abuse of the Stage. To omit these, however historically interesting they may be, is not to dim the reputation of their writer.

Neither does such omission obscure the principles he expounds. It may even be claimed that it exposes them, as good timber is exposed in a wood by the cutting away of the undergrowth. For what Dr. McAdoo remarks about Jeremy Taylor might well be applied to William Law—"against his unfortunate diffuseness in details may be set his decisiveness on principles".[1] Times change and literary fashions change. The spacious days in which Law lived afforded leisure for a type of writing, reading and of promiscuity in study which is lacking in our age of hurry. Streamlining has its present-day attraction in all departments of life, including literature. It is in order to keep this volume within reasonable limits of size and to bring Law within the orbit of those who have never acquired the art of leisurely reading, that I have committed what must appear to many of his admirers a sacrilege—abridgment. The whole point of it, however, is that it is an effort to introduce a unified Law, and not merely one aspect of his teaching, to the notice of those whose knowledge of him is, up to the present, one-sided, or even non-existent.

The widespread revival of interest in him and his work is a proof that his message is not obsolete; nor his cult just a matter of historical interest. But the revival takes strange shapes in concentrating on one aspect or another of his message to the exclusion of other aspects and so ignoring its wholeness, and consequently failing to recognise the manifold greatness of this English prophet, a prophet not only for the eighteenth century, but also for the twentieth. In an age in which there is a craze for snippets of learning,

[1] *The Structure of Caroline Moral Theology,* p. 43. (This book forms a useful preliminary to the study of William Law, revealing his writings in their true value and perspective as the development of a great tradition.)

and consecutive reading is at a discount, it is well to let Law speak for himself and to bear in mind his own *Advertisement to the Reader:*

> I have nothing to say by way of Preface or Introduction. I only ask this favour of the Reader, that he would not pass any censure on this book, from only dipping into this or that particular of it; but give it one fair perusal in the Order it is written; and then I shall have neither right nor inclination to complain of any judgment he shall think fit to pass upon it.

A. W. H.

Wareham, 1949

THE THREE BOOKS

15

A PRACTICAL TREATISE UPON CHRISTIAN PERFECTION

By WILLIAM LAW, M.A.

Not as though I had already attained, either were already perfect.—Phil. iii., 12.

(*Abridged*)

CONTENTS

I

I

CHRISTIAN Perfection will perhaps seem to the common reader to imply some state of life which everyone need not aspire after; that it is made up of such strictnesses, retirements and particularities of devotion as are neither necessary nor practicable by the generality of Christians.

But I must answer for myself that I know of only one common Christianity, which is to be the common means of salvation to all men.

If the writers upon Christian Perfection have fancied to themselves some peculiar degrees of piety, or extraordinary devotions which they call by that name, they have not done religion much service by making Christian Perfection to consist in anything but the right performance of our necessary duties.

This is the Perfection which this Treatise endeavours to recommend; a Perfection that does not consist in any singular state or condition of life, or in any particular set of duties, but in the holy and religious conduct of ourselves in every state of life. It calls no one to a cloister, but to a right and full performance of those duties which are necessary for all Christians, and common to all states of life.

I call it Perfection for two reasons: first, because I hope it contains a full representation of that height of holiness and purity to which Christianity calls all its members: secondly, that the Title may invite the reader to peruse it with the more diligence as expecting to find not only a discourse upon moral virtues, but a regular draught of those holy tempers which are the perfect measure and standard of Christian piety.

Now as Perfection is here placed in the right performance of our necessary duties, in the exercise of such holy tempers as are equally necessary and equally practicable in all states of life, as this is the highest degree of Christian Perfection, so it is to be observed that it is also the lowest degree of holiness which the Gospel alloweth. So that though no order of men can pretend to go higher, yet none of us can have any security in resting in any state of piety that is lower.

And I hope that it will be taken as a sign that I have hit upon the true state of Christian Perfection if I show it to be such as men in cloisters and religious retirements cannot add more, and at the same time, such as Christians in all states of the world must not be content with less.

For consider, what can Christian Perfection be but such a right performance of all the duties of life as is according to the laws of Christ? What can it be but a living in such holy tempers and acting with such dispositions as Christianity requires? Now if this be Perfection, who can exceed it? And yet what state or circumstance of life can allow any people to fall short of it?

Let us take an instance in some one particular temper of Christianity. Let it be the Love of God. Christians are to love God *with all their heart and all their strength*. Now can any order of Christians exceed in this temper? Or is there any order of Christians who may be allowed to be defective in it?

Now what is thus true of the Love of God is equally true of all other religious duties, and consequently all those holy tempers of heart which constitute the Perfection of Christian piety are tempers equally necessary for all Christians.

As there is but one faith and one Baptism, so there is but one Piety and one Perfection that is common to all orders of Christians. It will perhaps be here objected that this supposes that all people may be equally good, which seems as impossible in the nature of things as to suppose that all people may be equally wise. To this it may be answered that this is neither altogether true nor altogether false.

For to instance in Charity it is true that all people may be equally charitable, if we understand by Charity that habit of mind which stands rightly disposed to all acts of Charity. In this sense all people maybe equally charitable. But if we take Charity for Alms-giving, or a liberal assistance of the poor, in this sense it is false that all people may be equally charitable.

Now as it is the habit of the mind that constitutes the excellence of Charity, so this is the Charity to which Christians are called, and in which they may all be equally perfect.

Again, are not all people obliged to be equally honest, just, true, and faithful? In these virtues all are to be eminent and exact in the same degree. There are no abatements to be made for any rank or order of people. Now as to the external exercise of these duties there may be great difference. One man may have great business in the world and be honest and faithful in it all: another may have small dealings and be honest in them: but provided that there be in both of them the same justice and integrity of mind, they are equally honest; though their instances of honesty, as to external acts of it, are as different as great things are different from small. But as it is the habit of the mind which is the justice which Religion requires, so in this respect all people may be equally just.

Now this may serve to show us in what respect all people may be equally virtuous, and in what respect they cannot. As to the external instances or acts of virtue, in these they must differ according to the difference of their circumstances and condition in the world: but as virtues are considered as habits of the mind and principles of the heart, in this respect they may all be equally virtuous and are all called to the same Perfection.

A man cannot exercise the spirit of martyrdom till he is brought to the stake. He cannot forgive his enemies till they have done him wrong, till he suffers from them. He cannot bear poverty and distress till they are brought upon him. All these acts of virtue depend upon outward causes; but yet he may have a piety and heroic spirit equal to those who have died for their religion. He may have that charity of mind which prays for its enemies: he may have that meekness and resignation to the will of God as disposes people to bear poverty and distress with patience and humble submission to the Divine Providence.

So that they are only the external instances and acts of virtue which depend upon outward causes and circumstances of life. A man cannot give till he has something to give; but the inward piety of the heart and mind which constitutes the state of Christian Perfection depends upon no outward circumstances. A man need not want charity because he has no riches, nor be destitute of a forgiving spirit because he has no persecutors to forgive.

Although, therefore, we neither are nor can be all in the same circumstances of life, yet we are to be all in the same spirit of religion. Though we cannot all be equal in Almsgiving, yet we are to be all alike in Charity. Though we are not all in the same state of persecution, yet we must be all in the same spirit that forgives and prays for its persecutors. Though we are not all in poverty and distress, yet we must all be full of that piety of heart which produces meekness, patience, and thankfulness in distress and poverty.

We can hardly reconcile it with the divine goodness to give one man two talents and another five, unless we suppose that he is as high in his Master's pleasure who makes the right use of two as he that makes the right use of five talents. So that it still holds good that it is the Perfection of the heart that makes the Perfection of every state of life.

It may perhaps be further objected that the different degrees of glory in another life supposes that good men and such as are accepted of God do yet differ in their degrees of goodness in this life.

Now as it suits with the divine mercy to admit men to happiness who have not been in every respect so perfect as they might have been, notwithstanding that He gave them such a rule of Perfection; so it equally suits with the divine mercy to admit men to different degrees of happiness on account of their different conduct, though He gave them all one common rule of Perfection.

It therefore plainly appears that the different degrees of glory in another life are no more a proof that God calls some persons to different and lower states of goodness than others, than His pardoning variety of sinners is a proof that He allowed of those kinds of sin and did not require men to avoid them. For it is full as good an argument to say God pardons some sinners, therefore He did not require them to avoid such sins, as to say God rewards different degrees of goodness, therefore He did not call people to higher degrees of goodness. So that the different degrees of glory in the world to come are no objection against this doctrine that all Christians are called to one and the same piety and perfection of heart.

Lastly, it may be farther objected that although the law of God calls all men to the same state of Perfection, yet if there are different degrees of glory given to different degrees of goodness, this shows that men may be saved and happy without aspiring after all that Perfection to which they were called.

It may be answered that this is a false conclusion. For though it may be true that people will be admitted to happiness and different degrees of happiness, though they have not attained to all that Perfection to which they were called, yet it does not follow that any people will be saved who did not endeavour after that Perfection. For surely it is a very different case to fall short of our Perfection after our best endeavours, and to stop short of it by not endeavouring to arrive at it. The one practice may carry men to a high reward in Heaven, and the other cast them with the unprofitable servant into outer darkness.

God seeth different abilities and frailities in men, which may move His goodness to be merciful to their different improvements in virtue. I grant thee that there may be a lower state of piety which in some persons may be accepted by God. But consider that though there is such a state of piety that may be accepted, yet that it cannot be chosen. It ceases to be that state as soon as thou chooseth it.

God may be merciful to a low estate of piety by reason of some pitiable circumstances that may attend it but as soon as thou choosest such an estate of piety, it loses those pitiable circumstances and instead of a low state of piety is changed into a high state of impiety.

So that though there are meaner improvements in virtue which may make some persons accepted by God, yet this is no ground for content or satisfaction in such a state; because it ceases to be such a state, and is quite another thing, for being chosen and satisfied with.

It appears therefore from these considerations that notwithstanding God may accept of different degrees of goodness, and reward them with different degrees of glory in another life, yet that all Christians are called to one and the same Perfection, and equally obliged to labour after it.

This much may suffice to give the reader a general notion of Perfection and the necessity of endeavouring after it. What it is, and what holy tempers it requires will, I hope, be found sufficiently explained in the following chapters.

II

THE NATURE AND DESIGN OF CHRISTIANITY, THAT ITS SOLE
END IS TO DELIVER US FROM THE MISERY AND DISORDER OF
THIS PRESENT STATE, AND RAISE US TO A BLISSFUL ENJOYMENT
OF THE DIVINE NATURE

THE WISDOM of mankind has for several ages of the world
been enquiring into the nature of Man, and the nature of
the world in which he is placed.

The wants and miseries of human nature and the vanity
of worldly enjoyments has made it difficult for the wisest
men to tell what human happiness was, or wherein it
consisted.

It has pleased the infinite goodness of God to satisfy
all our wants and inquiries by a revelation made to the world
by His Son Jesus Christ. This revelation has laid open the
great secrets of Providence from the creation of the world,
explained the present state of things, and given man information that is necessary to quiet his anxieties, content
him with his condition, and lead him safely to everlasting
rest and happiness.

It is now only necessary that the poor wisdom of man
do not exalt itself against God, that we suffer our eyes to
be opened by Him that made them and our lives to be
conducted by Him in whom we live, move and have our
being. For Light is now come into the world if men are
but willing to come out of darkness.

As happiness is the sole end of all our labours, so this
Divine Revelation aims at nothing else. It gives us right
and satisfactory notions of ourselves, of our true and real
evil; it shows us the true state of our condition, both our
vanity and excellence, our greatness and meanness, our
felicity and misery.

Before this, man was a mere riddle to himself and his condition full of darkness and perplexity. A restless inhabitant of a miserable disordered world, *walking in a vain shadow and disquieting himself in vain*. But this Light has dispersed all the anxiety of his vain conjectures. It has brought us acquainted with God, and by adding Heaven to Earth, and Eternity to Time, has opened such a glorious view of things as makes man even in his present condition full of a Peace of God which passes all understanding.

This Revelation acquaints us that we have a spirit within us that was created after the Divine Image, that this spirit is now in a fallen corrupt condition, that the body in which it is placed is its grave or sepulchre where it is enslaved to fleshly thoughts, blinded with false notions of good and evil and dead to all taste and relish of its true happiness. It teaches us that the world in which we live is also in a disordered irregular state and cursed for the sake of man; that it is no longer the Paradise that God made it, but the remains of a drowned world, full of marks of God's displeasure and the sin of its inhabitants; that it is a mere wilderness, a place of darkness, a vale of misery, where vice and madness, dreams and shadows variously please, agitate, and torment the short miserable lives of men. Devils also, and evil spirits have here their residence, promoting the works of darkness and wandering up and down, seeking whom they may devour. So that the condition of man in his natural state seems to be as if a person sick of a variety of diseases, knowing neither his distempers nor his cure, should be enclosed in some place where he could hear or see or feel or taste of nothing but what tended to inflame his disorders.

The excellency therefore of the Christian Religion appears as this, that it puts an end to this state of things, blots out all the ideas of worldly wisdom, brings the world itself to ashes and creates all anew. It calls man from an animal life and earthly conversation to be born again of the

Holy Ghost and be made a member of the Kingdom of God. It does not leave us to grovel in the desires of the flesh, to cast about for worldly happiness and wander in darkness and exile from God, but prepares us for the true enjoyment of a divine life.

The manner by which it changes this whole state of things and raises us to an union with God is equally great and wonderful. *I am the Way, the Truth and the Life,* saith our Blessed Saviour, *no man cometh unto the Father but by me.*

As all things were at first created by the Son of God and without Him was not anything made that was made, so are all things again restored and redeemed by the same Divine Person. As nothing could come into being without Him, so nothing can enter into a state of happiness or enjoyment of God but by Him.

The price and dignity of this Redemption at once confounds the pride and relieves the misery of man. How fallen must he be from God, how disordered and odious his nature that should need so great a Mediator to recommend his repentance! And, on the other hand, how full of comfort that so high a method, so stupendous a means should be taken to restore him to a state of peace and favour with God!

This is the true point of view in which every Christian is to behold himself. He is to overlook the poor projects of human life and consider himself as a creature through his natural corruption falling into a state of endless misery, but by the mercy of God redeemed to a condition of everlasting felicity. All the precepts and doctrines of the Gospel are founded on these two great truths, the deplorable corruption of human nature and its new Birth in Christ Jesus.

The corruption of our nature makes mortification, self-denial, and the death of our bodies necessary, because human nature must be thus unmade, flesh and blood must be thus changed, before it can enter into the Kingdom of Heaven. Our new Birth makes the reception of God's Spirit and the participation of the Holy Sacraments necessary to form us to that life to which the Resurrection of Jesus Christ has entitled us. So that would we think and act and live like Christians, we must act suitably to these terms of our condition, fearing and avoiding all the motions of our corrupted nature, cherishing the secret inspirations of the Holy Spirit, opening our minds for the reception of the Divine Light and pressing after the graces and perfections of our new Birth.

The Christian State is an invisible life in the Spirit of God, supported not by sensible goods, but the spiritual graces of Faith and Hope; so that the natural man, especially while busied in earthly cares and enjoyments, easily forgets that great and heavenly condition in which religion places him.

The changes which Christianity maketh in the present state of things are all invisible, its goods and evils, its dignities and advantages, which are the only true standards of all our actions, are not subject to the knowledge of our senses. In God *we live and move and have our being,* but how unseen, how unfelt it all is!

Christ is the *Lamb slain from the foundation of the world,* the True Light that lighteth every man that cometh into the world. He is the Alpha and Omega, the Beginning and End of all things. The whole Creation subsists in Him and by Him. Nothing is in any order, nor any person in any favour with God but by this great Mediator. But how invisible, how unknown to all our senses in this state of things!

Religion turns our whole life into a sacrifice to God, a state of probation from which we must *all appear before the Judgement-Seat of Christ, that everyone may receive the things done in his body.* But our senses, the maxims of this life,

and the spirit of the world, teach quite another turn of
mind; to enjoy the good things of life as our portion, to
seek after riches and honours, and to dread nothing so
much as poverty, disgrace and persecution. Well may this
life be deemed a state of darkness since it thus clouds and
covers all the true appearances of things and keeps our
minds insensible and unaffected with matters of such infinite
moment.

We must observe that in Scripture Christianity is
constantly represented to us as a Redemption from the
slavery and corruption of our nature, and a raising us to a
nearer enjoyment of the Divine Glory. Christianity is so
divine in its nature, so noble in its ends, so extensive in
its views that it has no lesser subjects than these to entertain
our thoughts. It buries our bodies, burns the present world,
triumphs over Death by a general Resurrection and opens
all into an eternal state. It never considers us in any other
respect than as fallen spirits. It disregards the distinctions
of human society and proposes nothing to our fears but
eternal misery, nor anything to our hopes but an endless
enjoyment of the divine nature.

This is the great and important condition in which
Christianity has placed us, above our bodies, above the
world, above death, to be present at the dissolution of all
things, to see the earth in flames and the heavens wrapt
up like a scroll, to stand at the general Resurrection, to
appear at the universal Judgment, and to live for ever when
all that our eyes have seen is passed away and gone.

Take upon thee therefore a spirit and temper suitable
to this greatness of thy condition. Remember that thou
art an eternal spirit, that thou art for a few months and
years in a state of flesh and blood only to try whether thou
shalt be for ever happy with God, or fall into everlasting
misery with the devil.

Thou wilt often hear of other concerns and other greatness in the world. Thou wilt see every order of men, every

family, every person pursuing some fancied happiness of his own as if the world had not only happiness, but a particular kind of happiness for all its inhabitants. But when thou seest this state of human life, fancy that thou sawest all the world asleep, the prince no longer a prince, the beggar no longer begging, but every man sleeping out of his proper state, some happy, some tormented and all changing their condition as fast as one foolish dream could succeed another. When thou hast seen this thou hast seen all that the world awake can do for thee. If thou wilt thou mayst go to sleep for awhile, thou mayst lie down and dream; for, be as happy as the world can make thee, all is but sleeping and dreaming, and what is still worse, it is like sleeping in a ship when thou shouldst be pumping out the water, or dreaming thou art a prince when thou shouldst be redeeming thyself from slavery.

Now this is no imaginary flight of a melancholy fancy that too much exceeds the nature of things, but a sober reflection justly suited to the vanity of worldly enjoyments. For if the doctrines of Christianity are true, if thou art that creature, that fallen spirit, that immortal nature which Religion teaches us, if thou art to meet Death, Resurrection and Judgment as the forerunners of an eternal state, what are all the little flashes of pleasure, the changing appearances of worldly felicities but so many sorts of dreams? How canst thou talk of the happiness of riches, the advantages of fortune, the pleasures of apparel, of state and equipage without being in a dream? Is the beggar asleep when he fancies he is building himself fine houses? Is the prisoner in a dream when he imagines himself in open fields and fine groves? And canst thou think that thy immortal spirit is awake whilst it is delighting itself in the shadows and bubbles of worldly happiness?

For if it be true that man is upon his trial, if the trial is for Eternity, if life is but a vapour, what is there that deserves a serious thought but how to get well out of the world, and make it a right passage to our eternal state? How can we prove that we are awake, that our eyes are open, but by seeing and feeling and living according to these important circumstances of our life.?

If a man should endeavour to please thee with fine descriptions of the riches and pleasures and dignities of the world in the moon, adding that its air is always serene and its seasons always pleasant, would'st thou not think it a sufficient answer to say, I am not to live there? When thy own false heart is endeavouring to please itself with worldly expectations, the joy of this or that way of life, is it not as good a reproof to say to thyself, I am not to stay there? For where is the difference betwixt an earthly happiness from which thou art to be separated for ever and a happiness in the moon to which thou art never to go? Thou art to be for ever separated from the earth, thou art to be eternal, when the earth itself is lost; is it not therefore the same vanity to project for happiness on earth as to propose a happiness in the moon? For as thou art never to go to the one, so thou art to be eternally separated from the other.

Every man sees the littleness of all sorts of honours but those which he is looking after himself. A private English gentleman that is half distracted till he has got some little distinction does at the same time despise the highest honours of other countries, and would not leave his own condition to possess the ridiculous greatness of an Indian King. He sees the vanity and falseness of their honours, but forgets that all honour placed in external things is equally vain and false. He does not consider that the difference of greatness is only the difference of flowers and feathers, and that they who are dressing themselves with beads have as just a taste of what adorns their persons as they who place the same pride in diamonds. When we read of an Eastern Prince that is too great to feed himself and thinks it a piece of grandeur to have other people put his meat into his mouth, we despise the folly of his pride. But might we not as well despise the folly of their pride who are ashamed to use their legs and think it adds to their state to be removed from one place to another by other people. For he that thinks it stately to be carried, and mean to walk on foot, has as true notions of greatness as he who is too haughty to put his meat in his own month.

Again, it is the manner of some countries in the burial of their dead to put a staff and shoes and money in the sepulchre along with the corpse. We justly censure the folly and ignorance of such a poor contrivance to assist the dead, but if we did but truly understand what life is, we should see as much to ridicule in the poor contrivances to assist the living. For how many things in life do people labour after, break their rest and peace to get, which yet when gotten are of as much real use to them as a staff and shoes to a corpse under ground? They are always adding something to their life which is only like adding another pair of shoes to a body in the grave. Thou mayst hire more servants, new paint thy rooms, make more fine beds, eat out of plate and put on richer apparel, and these will help thee to be happy as golden staves or painted shoes will help a dead man to walk.

See here therefore the true nature of all worldy show and figure: it will make us as great as those are who are dreaming that they are kings, as rich as those who fancy that they have estates in the moon, and as happy as those who are buried with staves in their hands. So that he who condemns all the external show and state of life as equally vain is no more deceived, or carried to too high a contempt for the things of this life than he that only condemns the vanity of the vainest things.

Do but therefore know thyself as religion has made thee known, do but see thyself in the light which Christ has brought into the world, and then thou wilt see that nothing concerns thee but what concerns an everlasting spirit that is going to God: and that there are no enjoyments here that are worth a thought but such as may make thee more perfect in those holy tempers which will carry thee to Heaven.

III

CHRISTIANITY REQUIRES A CHANGE OF NATURE: A NEW LIFE PERFECTLY DEVOTED TO GOD

CHRISTIANITY is not a school for the teaching of moral virtue, the polishing our manners, or forming us to live a life of this world with decency and gentility. It is deeper and more divine in its designs and has much nobler ends than these. It implies an entire change of life, a dedication of ourselves, our souls and bodies unto God in the strictest and highest sense of the words.

Our Blessed Saviour came into the world not to make any composition with it, or to divide things between Heaven and Earth, but to make war with every state of life, to put an end to the designs of flesh and blood, and to show us that we must either leave this world to become Sons of God, or by enjoying it, take our portion amongst Devils and damned Spirits.

Death is not more certainly a separation of our souls from our bodies than the Christian life is a separation of our souls from worldly tempers, vain indulgences, and unnecessary cares.

No sooner are we baptized but we are to consider ourselves as new and holy persons that are entered upon a new state of things, that are devoted to God and have renounced all to be fellow-heirs with Christ and members of His Kingdom.

There is no alteration of life, no change of condition that implies half so much as that alteration which Christianity introduceth. It is a Kingdom of Heaven begun upon earth and by being made members of it we are entered into a new state of goods and evils. Eternity altereth the face and nature of everything in this world. Life is only a trial, prosperity becometh adversity, pleasure a mischief, and nothing a good; but as it increaseth our hope, purifieth our natures and prepareth us to receive higher degrees of happiness.

Let us now see what it is to enter into this State of Redemption.

Our own Church in conformity with Scripture and the practice of the purest ages makes it necessary for us to renounce the Pomps and Vanities of the World before we can be received as members of Christian Communion. Did we enough consider this we should find that whenever we yield ourselves up to the pleasures, profits and honours of this life that we turn apostates, break our covenant with God and go back from the express conditions on which we were admitted into the Communion of Christ's Church.

If we consult either the life or doctrines of our Saviour we shall find that Christianity is a Covenant that contains only the terms of changing and resigning this world for another that is to come. It is a state of things that wholly regards Eternity and knows of no other goods and evils but such as relate to another life. It is a Kingdom of Heaven that has no other interests in this world than as it takes its members out of it.

To return: Christianity is therefore a course of Holy Disipline solely fitted to the cure and recovery of fallen spirits, and intends such a change in our nature as may raise us to a nearer union with God and qualify us for such high degrees of happiness.

That Christianity requires a change of nature, a new life perfectly devoted to God is plain from the spirit and tenor of the Gospel. The Saviour of the word saith *that except a man be born again, of the Water and the Spirit, he cannot enter into the Kingdom of God.* These words plainly teach us that Christianity implies some great change of nature, that as our birth was to us the beginning of a new life and brought us into a society of earthly enjoyments, so Christianity is another birth that brings us into a condition altogether as new as when we first saw the Light. We begin again to be, we enter upon fresh terms of life, have new relations, new hopes and fears and an entire change of everything that can be called good or evil.

This new birth, this principle of a new life, is the very essence and soul of Christianity. It is a seal of the promises, a mark of our sonship, the earnest of the inheritance, the security of our hope and the foundation of all our acceptance with God. *He that is in Christ,* saith the Apostle, *is a new Creature, and if any Man hath not the Spirit of Christ, he is none of his.* And again, *He who is joined to the Lord is one Spirit.*

It is not therefore any number of moral virtues, no partial obedience, no modes of worship, no external acts of adoration, no articles of faith but a new principle of life, and entire change of temper that makes us true Christians.

St. John tells us one sure mark of our new Birth in the following words, *He that is born of God overcometh the world.* So that the new birth, or the Christian life is considered with opposition to the world and all that is in it, its vain cares, its false glories, proud designs and sensual pleasures. If we have overcome these so as to be governed by other cares, other glories, other designs and other pleasures, then are we born of God. Then is the wisdom of this world and the friendship of this world turned into the wisdom and friendship of God, which will for ever keep us heirs of God and joint-heirs with Christ.

Again, the same Apostle helps us to another Sign of our new Life in God. *Whosoever,* saith he, *is born of God, doth not commit sin, for his seed remaineth in him and he cannot sin because he is born of God.* This is not to be understood as if he that were born of God was therefore in an absolute state of Perfection, and incapable afterwards of falling into anything that was sinful. It only means that he that is born of God is possessed of a temper and principle that makes him utterly hate and labour to avoid all sin. He is therefore said not to commit sin in such a sense as a man may be said not to do that which it is his constant care and principle to avoid being done.

We have already seen two marks of those that are born of God, the one is that they have overcome the world, the other that they do not commit sin. To these I shall only add a third which is given to us by Christ himself, *I say unto you, love your enemies, bless them that curse you, do good to them that hate you, and pray for them which despitefully use you and persecute you, that you may be the Children of your Father which is in Heaven.*

Let us here awhile contemplate the height and depth of Christian holiness and that god-like spirit which our religion requireth. This duty of Universal Love and Benevolence, even to our bitterest enemies, may serve to convince us that to be Christians we must be *born again,* change our very natures, and have no governing desire of our souls but that of being made like God. The same doctrine is farther taught by our blessed Saviour when speaking of little children, he saith *Suffer them to come unto me, for of such is the Kingdom of God.* And again, *Whosoever shall not receive the Kingdom of God as a little child shall in no wise enter therein.*

If we are not resolved to deceive ourselves, to have eyes and see not, ears and hear not, we must perceive that these words imply some mighty change in our nature. For what can make us more contrary to ourselves than to lay aside all our manly wisdom, our mature judgments, our boasted abilities and become infants in nature and temper before we can partake of this heavenly state? We reckon it change enough from babes to be men, and surely it must signify as great an alteration to be reduced from men to a state of infancy. One peculiar condition of infants is this, that they have everything to learn, they are to be taught by others what they are to hope and fear, and wherein their proper happiness consists. It is in this sense that we are chiefly to become as infants, to be as though that we had everything to learn, and suffer ourselves to be taught what we are to choose and what to avoid: to pretend to no wisdom of our own, but be ready to pursue that happiness which God in Christ proposes to us, and to accept it with such simplicity of mind, as children that have nothing of our own to oppose to it.

But now, is this infant-temper thus essential to the Christian Life? Does the Kingdom of God consist only of such as are so affected? Let this then be added as another undeniable proof that Christianity requires a new nature and temper of mind, and that this temper is such as having renounced the prejudices of life, the maxims of human wisdom, yields itself with a child-like submission and simplicity to be entirely governed by the precepts and doctrines of Christ. Craft and policy, selfish cunning, proud abilities and vain endowments have no admittance into this holy state of society with Christ and God. The wisdom of this world, the intrigues of life, the designs of greatness and ambition, lead to another Kingdom, and he that would follow Christ must empty himself of this vain furniture, and put on the meek ornaments of infant and undesigning simplicity.

The Holy Spirit of God is not satisfied with representing that change which Christianity introduceth by telling us that it is a new birth, a being born of God and the like, but proceeds to convince us of the same truth by another way of speaking, by representing it as a State of Death. Thus saith the Apostle, *ye are dead, and your life is hid with Christ*

in God. That is, you Christians are dead as to this world and
the life which you now live is not to be reckoned by any
visible or worldly goods, but is hid in Christ, is a spiritual
enjoyment, a life of faith and not of sight: ye are members
of that Mystical Body of which Christ is the Head, and
entered into a Kingdom which is not of this world. And
in this state of death are we as Christians to continue till
*Christ who is our life, shall appear, and then shall we also appear
with him in glory.*

To show us that this Death begins with our Christian
State, we are said to be *buried with him in Baptism*; so that
we entered into this State of Death at our Baptism, when
we entered into Christianity. *Know ye not*, saith the Apostle,
*that so many of us as were baptized into Jesus Christ were baptized
into his Death? Therefore we are buried with him, by Baptism
unto Death.*

Now Christians may be said to be baptized into the
Death of Christ if their Baptism puts them into a state like
to that in which our Saviour was at His Death. The Apostle
shows us this to be the meaning of it by saying *if we have
been planted together in the likeness of his Death*, that is, if
our Baptism has put us into a state like that of His Death.
So that Christian Baptism is not only an external rite by
which we are entered into the external society of
Christ's Church, but is a solemn consecration which
presents us an offering to God, as Christ was offered at
His Death.

We are therefore no longer alive to the enjoyments of
this world, but as Christ was then nailed to the Cross and
devoted entirely to God, that he might be made *perfect
through sufferings* and ascend to the right hand of God, so
is our old man to be crucified and we consecrated to God by
a conformity to the death of Christ, that *like as Christ was
raised from the Dead by the Glory of the Father, even so we also
should walk in newness of Life*, and *being risen with Christ,
should seek those things which are above.*

This is the true undeniable state of Christianity. Baptism does not make us effectually Christians unless it brings us into a state of death, consecrates us to God, and begins a life suitable to that state of things to which our Saviour is risen from the dead. This, and no other than this, is the holiness and spiritual temper of the Christian life which implies such a resignation of mind, such a dedication of ourselves to God, as may resemble the death of Christ; and on the other hand, such a newness of life, such an ascension of the soul, such a holy and heavenly behaviour as may show that we are risen with Christ and belong to that glorious state where he now sits at the right hand of God.

We must then, if we would be wise unto Salvation, die and rise again like Christ and make all the actions of our life holy by offering them to God. *Whether we eat or drink, or whatsoever we do, we must do all to the Glory of God.*

Since then he that is called to Christianity is thus called to an imitation of the death of Christ, to forbear from sin, to overcome the world, to be born of the Spirit, to be born of God; these surely will be allowed to be sufficient evidences that Christianity requireth an entire change of our nature, a life perfectly devoted to God.

Now if this is Christian piety it may serve to instruct two sorts of people. First, those who are content with an outward decency and regularity of life. I don't mean such as are hypocritical in their virtues, but all those who are content with an outward form of behaviour without that inward newness of heart and spirit which the Gospel requireth.

Charity, Chastity, Sobriety and Justice may be practised without Christian Piety. A Jew, a heathen may be charitable and temperate; but to make these virtues become parts of Christian Piety they must proceed from a heart truly turned unto God, that is full of an infant simplicity, that is crucified with Christ, that is born again of the Spirit, that has overcome the world. Temperance or Justice without this turn of heart may be the temperance of a Jew or a heathen, but it is not Christian Temperance till it proceed from a true Christian spirit. Could we do or suffer all that Christ himself did or suffered, yet if it was not done in the same spirit and temper of Christ we should have none of His merit.

A Christian therefore must be sober, charitable and just, upon the same principles and with the same spirit that he receives the Holy Sacrament, for ends of religion, as acts of obedience to God, as means of purity and holiness and as so many instances of a heart devoted to God. As the bare eating of Bread and drinking Wine in the Holy Sacrament is of no use to us without those religious dispositions which constitute the true frame of a pious mind; so is it the same in all other duties. They are mere outward ceremonies and useless actions unless they are performed in the spirit of Religion. Charity and sobriety are of no value till they are so many instances of a heart devoted to God.

A Christian therefore is to be sober not only so far as answers the ends of a decent and orderly life, but in such a manner as becomes one who is born of the Holy Spirit, that is made one with Christ, who dwells in Christ and Christ in him. He must be sober in such a measure as best serves the ends of religion, and practise such an abstinence as may make him fittest for the holiness, purity and perfection of the Christian Life. He must be charitable not so far as suits with humanity and good esteem amongst men, but in such a measure as is according to the doctrines and spirit of Religion. For neither charity nor temperance nor any other virtue are parts of Christian holiness till they are made holy and religious by such a piety of heart as shows that we live wholly unto God.

This is what cannot be too much considered by a great many people whose religion has made no change in their hearts, but only consists in an external decency of life, who are sober without the piety of sobriety, who pray without devotion, who give alms without charity, and are Christians without the spirit of Christianity. Let them remember that religion is to alter our nature, that Christian piety consists in a change of heart, that it implies a new turn of spirit, a spiritual death, a spiritual life, a dying to the world, and a living wholly unto God.

Secondly, this doctrine may serve to instruct those who have lived strangers to religion, what they are to do to become true Christians. Some people who are ashamed of the folly of their lives and begin to look towards religion, think they have done enough when they either alter the outward course of their lives, abate some of their extravagances, or become careful of some particular virtue. Thus a man whose life has been a course of folly thinks he has made a sufficient change by becoming temperate. Another imagines he has sufficiently declared for religion by not neglecting the Public Worship as he used to do. A lady fancies that she lives unto God because she has left off plays and paint, and lives more at home than in the former part of her life. But such people should consider that religion is no one particular virtue, that it does not consist in the fewness of our vices, or in any particular amendment of our lives, but in such a thorough change of heart as makes piety and holiness the measure and rule of all our tempers.

It is a miserable error to be content with ourselves because we are less vain, or covetous, more sober and decent in our behaviour than we used to be. Yet this is the state of many people who think that they have sufficiently reformed their lives because they are in some degree different from what they were. They think it enough to be changed from what they were, without considering how thorough a change religion requires.

Let us therefore look carefully to ourselves and consider what manner of spirit we are of. Let us not think our condition safe because we are of this or that Church or Communion, or because we are strict observers of the external offices of religion, for these are marks that belong to more than belong to Christ. All are not His that prophesy or even work miracles in His Name, much less those who with worldly minds and corrupt hearts are only baptized in His Name.

If religion has raised us into a new world, if it has filled us with new ends of life, if it has taken possession of our hearts, and altered the whole turn of our minds, if it has changed all our ideas of things, given us a new set of hopes and fears, and taught us to live by the realities of an invisible world; then may we humbly hope that we are true followers of the Holy Jesus, and such as may rejoice in the Day of Christ that we have neither run in vain nor laboured in vain.

IV

CHRISTIANITY REQUIRETH A RENUNCIATION OF THE WORLD, AND OF ALL WORLDLY TEMPERS

THE Christian Religion being to raise a new, spiritual and as yet invisible world, and to place a man in a certain order amongst Thrones, Principalities and Spiritual Beings, is at entire enmity with this present corrupt state of flesh and blood. It ranks the present world along with the flesh and the Devil as an equal enemy to those glorious ends, and that perfection of human nature which our Redemption proposes.

The wisdom of this world gives an importance and air of greatness to several ways of life, and ridicules others as vain and contemptible, which differ only in their kind of vanity. But the wisdom from above condemns all labour as equally fruitless but that which labours after everlasting

life. Let but religion determine the point, and what can it
signify whether a man forgets God in his farm, or a shop,
or at a gaming-table? For the world is full as great and
important in its pleasures as in its cares. There is no more
wisdom in the one than in the other, and the Christian
that is governed by either and made less affected to things
of God by them is equally odious and contemptible in the
sight of God.

For this reason our Lord points his doctrines at the most
common and allowed enjoyments of life, to teach us that
they may employ our minds as falsely, and distract us as far
from our true good as any trifles and vanity. He calls us
from such cares to convince us that even the necessities
of life must be sought with a kind of indifference, that so
our souls may be truly sensible of greater wants and disposed to hunger and thirst after enjoyments that will make
us happy for ever.

But how unlike are Christians to Christianity!

I know it is pretended by some that these doctrines of our
Saviour concerning forsaking all, and the like, related only
to his first followers, who could be his disciples upon no
other terms, and who were to suffer with him for the
propagation of the Gospel.

It is readily owned that there are different states of the
Church, and that such different states may call Christians
to some particular duties not common to every age. It
is owned also that this was the case of the first Christians,
they differed from us in many respects. They were personally called to follow Christ. They received particular
commissions from His mouth. They were empowered
to work miracles and called to a certain expectation of
hatred and sufferings from almost all the world. These are
particulars in which the state of the first Church differed
from the present.

But then it is carefully to be observed that this difference
in the state of the Church is a difference in the external

state of the Church, and not in the internal inward state of Christians. It is a difference that relates to the affairs and condition of the world and not to the personal holiness and purity of Christians.

Whatever degrees therefore of personal holiness or inward Perfection were required of the first followers of Christ is still in the same degree and for the same reasons required of all Christians to the end of the world.

Humility, Meekness, Heavenly Affection, Devotion, Charity and a Contempt of the World are all internal qualities of personal holiness. They constitute that spirit and temper of religion which is required for its own excellence and is therefore of constant and eternal obligation. There is always the same fitness and reasonableness in them, the same Perfection in practising of them and the same rewards always due to them.

If this be true, then it must be owned that it is still the same necessary duty and is now as well that proper behaviour of those who are the sons of God as ever it was. For Christianity is just that same spiritual heavenly state that it was then, the dignity of Christians has suffered no alteration since that time, and a treasure in Heaven, an eternal happiness are still the same great and important things.

I have, I think, sufficiently shown that our Saviour required an entire renunciation of the world, a forsaking all its enjoyments in order to be His true disciples, and that the same is as certainly required of us, as He is the same Christ and we heirs of the same glory.

It will now therefore I know be asked whether all Christians are obliged to sell their estates and give to the poor in order to inherit eternal life. The absurdity and ridiculousness of such a thing, and the disorder it must occasion in life, will be thought sufficient to expose and confute all the foregoing doctrine. As to the absurdity and ridiculousness of this doctrine in the eyes of worldly wisdom, that is far from being any objection against it, since we are assured by God himself that the wisdom of this world is foolishness with God, and that the spirit of Christianity and the spirit of the World are as contrary to one another as the Kingdom of Light and the Kingdom of Darkness.

What can be more contrary to worldly greatness and wisdom than the doctrine of the cross, a crucified Saviour? Which way could anyone expose himself to more jest and ridicule than by being too meek and humble to resent an affront and accept a challenge?

Not only rakes and libertines, but the grave, the religious part of the world talk of the necessity of defending their honour, and reckon it a shame not to resent and fight when the affront is given. This makes the spirit of the World, though it be as consistent with our religion, to honour the memory of Cain for killing his brother as to make it a part of honour to give or accept a challenge. This may serve to show us that we must disregard the maxims and wisdom of this world, and not form our judgments of Christian virtues with any regard to it since by it patience and meekness may be reckoned shameful, and revenge and murder as instances of honour.

I will now a little appeal to the imagination of the reader.

Let it be supposed that rich men are now enjoying their riches, and taking all the common usual delights of plenty; that they are labouring for the meat that perisheth, projecting and contriving scenes of pleasure and spending their estates in proud expenses. After this supposition let it be imagined that we saw the Holy Jesus, who had not where to lay His head, with His twelve Apostles that had left all to follow Him. Let us imagine that we heard Him call all the world to take up the Cross and follow Him, promising a Treasure in Heaven to such as would quit all for His sake, and rejecting all that would not comply with such terms, denouncing woe and eternal death to all that lived in fulness, pomp and worldly delights. Let it be imagined that we heard Him commanding His disciples to take no thought saying, What shall we eat, or What shall we drink, or Wherewithal shall we be clothed?—and giving this reason for it, because *after all these things do the Gentiles seek.*

Let it be imagined that we saw the first Christians taking up the Cross, renouncing the World and counting all but dung that they might gain Christ.

I do not now appeal to the judgment or reason of the reader, I leave it with his imagination, that wild faculty, to determine whether it be possible for these two different sorts of men to be true disciples of the same Lord.

To proceed. Let us suppose that a rich man was to put up such a prayer as this to God. "O Lord, I thy sinful creature who am born again to a lively hope of glory in Christ Jesus, beg of Thee to grant me a thousand times more riches than I need that I may be able to gratify myself and family in the delights of eating and drinking, state and grandeur, grant that as the little span of life wears out I may still abound more and more in wealth, and that I may see and perceive all the best and surest ways of growing richer than any of my neighbours: this I humbly and fervently beg in the Name, etc."

Such a Prayer as this should have had no place in this treatise but that I have reason to hope that in proportion as it offends the ear, it will amend the heart. There is no one, I believe, but would be ashamed to put up such a prayer as this to God yet let it be well observed that all are of the temper of this prayer, but those who have overcome the world.

We need not go amongst villains and people of scandalous characters to find out those who desire a thousand times more than they want, who have an eagerness to be every day richer and richer, who catch at all the ways of gain

THE POCKET WILLIAM LAW 47

that are not scandalous, and who hardly think anything enough except it equals or exceeds the estate of their neighbours. I beg of such that they would heartily condemn the profane and unchristian spirit of the foregoing prayer, that they would satisfy themselves that nothing can be more odious and contrary to religion than such petitions. But then let them be assured also of this, that the same things which make an unchristian prayer make an unchristian life.

From all that has been observed I think it is sufficiently plain that the present disciples of Jesus Christ are to have no more to do with worldly enjoyments than those that He chose whilst He himself was on earth, and that He expects as much devotion to God, and heavenly affection from us, as from any that He conversed with, and speaks the same language and gives the same commands to all rich men now that He gave to the rich young man in the Gospel.

Thus does it appear, from almost every part of Scripture, that a Renunciation of the world and all worldly enjoyments, either of pleasure or pride, is the necessary temper of all Christians of every state and condition.

I know that to all this it will still be objected that the different states of life are things indifferent in themselves, and are made good or evil by the tempers of the persons who enjoy them. That a man is not necessarily vain and proud because he lives in great show and figure any more than another is necessarily humble and lowly in mind because he lives in a low estate.

It is granted that men may be of a temper contrary to the state in which they live, but then this is only true of such as are in any state by force, and contrary to their desires and endeavours. A man in a low estate may be very vain and proud because he is in such a state by force, and is restless and uneasy till he can raise himself out of it. If the same can be said of any man that lives in all the splendour and figure of life, that he is in it by force, and is restless and uneasy till he can lay all aside and live in a humble lowly state, it may be granted that such a man, though in the height of figure, may be as humble as another in starving circumstances may be proud.

Again, those who talk of people being humble in a state that has all the appearance of pride and vanity, do not enough consider the nature of virtue. Humility and every other virtue is never in a complete state so that a man can say that he has finished his task in such or such a virtue. No virtues have any existence of this kind in human minds. They are rather continual struggles with the contrary vices than any finished habits of mind.

A man is humble, not for what he has already done, but because it is his continual disposition to oppose and reject every temptation to pride. Charity is a continual struggle with the contrary qualities of self-love and envy. And this is the state of every virtue, it is a progressive temper of mind, and always equally labouring to preserve itself.

V

CHRISTIANITY CALLETH ALL MEN TO A STATE OF SELF-DENIAL AND MORTIFICATION

CHRISTIANITY is a Doctrine of the Cross that teaches the restoration of mankind to the favour of God by the death and sacrifice of Jesus Christ. This being the foundation of the Christian Religion it shows us that all persons who will act comformably to the nature and reason of Christianity must make themselves sufferers for sin. For if there is a reasonableness between sin and suffering, every Christian acts against the reason of things that does not endeavour to pay some part of that debt which is due to sin. Indeed, it would be strange to suppose that mankind were redeemed by the sufferings of their Saviour, to live in ease and softness themselves; that suffering should be necessary atonement for sin and yet that sinners should be excused from sufferings.

Such an High Priest became us, says the Apostle, *who is holy, harmless, undefiled, separate from sinners.* Now if the holiness of Christ rendered His sacrifice acceptable to God does not this teach us that we must labour to be holy in order to be accepted of God? But is there not the same reason and the same example in the sufferings of Christ, if they made God more propitious to sin, must we not as well take this way of suffering to make ourselves fitter objects of Divine pardon?

There is therefore the same reason in the nature of the thing for us sinners to endeavour to conform ourselves to the sufferings, as to labour after the holiness of Christ, since they both jointly conspired to recommend the great Atonement for sin, and must jointly conspire to render us proper objects of the benefits of it. He that can doubt of this must suppose that God required a way of Atonement in Jesus Christ that had nothing of Atonement in it, for if it had it must be undeniable that all who, as far as their natures will allow, conform themselves to the similitude of Christ's sacrifice, must make themselves more acceptable to God.

That Christ's sufferings have not made all other sufferings for sin needless is plain from hence, that all Christians are still left subject to death. For surely it may be with truth affirmed that death is a suffering for sin.

Now since all Christians are to offer up their bodies at death as a sacrifice or suffering for sin, this plainly teaches us that a state of self-denial and suffering is the proper state of this life. For surely it must be proper to make every part of our life suitable to such an end.

Thus as the mortality of our condition is a certain proof

that our life is in disorder and unacceptable to God, so
is it also a proof that we ought to refuse pleasures and
satisfactions which are the pleasures of a state of disorder,
and stay for joy and delights till we are removed to such a
state of Perfection as God will delight to continue to all
eternity. If we consider that we are devoted to death, and
under a necessity of falling into dust as a sacrifice for sin,
does not this teach us the necessity of making our life
conformable to the intention of such a death? For could
there be any necessity that we should die as a sacrifice
for sin, if we might lead a life of a contrary nature? Or
could we act more contrary to God than by making that
life a state of pleasure and indulgence, which He has laid
under the curse of death? Ought we to indulge a life which
God considers as too unholy to continue in being?

Lastly, if we consider that repentance is the chief, the
most constant and perpetual duty of a Christian, that our
holiness has hardly any other existence than what arises
from a perpetual repentance, can it be doubted that
Mortification and Self-denial are essential, perpetual parts
of our duty? For to suppose a repentance without the pain
of Mortification and the punishment of Self-denial is as
absurd as to suppose a labour after holiness which takes
not one step towards it.

The whole matter, therefore, plainly comes to this, if
our sufferings, our injuries, or hardships be such as we
undergo because we dare not depart from that meekness
and patience and charity which Christ has taught, because
we had rather love our enemies than be revenged on them,
rather suffer like Christ and be full of His Spirit than avoid
sufferings by a contrary temper, such sufferings are our
greatest gains.

Before I proceed any further in other instances of Self-
denial, it may be proper to show in what the duty of Self-
denial is founded, or wherein the reasonableness and
necessity of it consists. Every duty or virtue of the

Christian Life is founded in truth and reason, and is required because of its fitness to be done, and not because God has power to command what He pleases. If we are commanded to be meek and humble, it is because meekness and humility are as true judgments and as suitable to the truth of our state as it is a true judgment and suitable to the state of every dependent Being to be thankful for mercies. If we are bid to rejoice, it is at something that is truly joyful. If to fear, it is to fear something that is really dreadful. Thus we are called to no tempers but such as are so many true judgments, and as well founded in the nature and reason of things as if we were bid to believe two to be the half part of four.

God is Reason and Wisdom itself, and He can no more call us to any tempers or duties but such as are strictly reasonable in themselves, than He can act against himself or contradict His own nature. As we can say with assurance that God cannot lie, so we may with the same certainty affirm that He cannot enjoin anything to rational creatures that is contrary to the reason of their nature, no more than He can enjoin them to love things that are not lovely, or hate things that are in their nature not hateful.

Again, God is Goodness itself, if therefore human goodness is inclined to endeavour the cure of madmen and fools must not Goodness itself be much more inclined to correct the madness and folly of fallen man? We see that men are said to be mad when they fancy themselves and the things about them to be different from what they are. They are said to be fools when they mistake the value of things. Now if this be true, as it most certainly is, it may serve to show us that man in his present state of disorder and ignorance must appear to God as both fool and mad; for every sinner is truly made as he imagines himself, and all things about him to be what they are not. He is really a fool as he is ridiculous to his choices, and mistakes the value of things.

Now Religion is our cure. It is God's merciful communication of such rules and discipline of life as may serve to deliver us from the infatuation and ignorance of our fallen state. It is to teach us the knowledge of ourselves, and all things about us, that we may no longer act like madmen. It is to teach us the true value of things that we may know our good and evil, and not be as idiots in the choice of things.

Now fools and madmen have their Paradise and are pleased with their imaginary happiness. This makes them averse from all methods of cure. For this reason, God presses His instructions upon us with terrors and threatenings, and makes those virtues which are the natural good and cure of our souls such duties to Him as He will punish the neglect of them. So that the power of God is mercifully employed to move us to such a reasonable Way of Life as is necessary for our happiness. Some people are so weak as to wonder what we call sin should be so odious to God, or what it can signify to God whether we are wise or foolish. Let such consider that God is Wisdom and Reason itself, and consequently everything that is contrary to reason and wisdom is contrary to His Nature, so that a state of sin is a state of contrariety to God. To ask therefore why God hates all sin is the same thing as to ask why God cannot tell any sort of lie. It is because every deviation from truth is contrary to His nature, which is Truth itself, so every instance of sin, as it is an unreasonable act, is contrary to His nature who is Reason itself.

There is therefore a necessity from the nature of things that every creature be delivered from sin before it can enter into the beatific Presence of God, for if God could reward wicked beings and make them happy by the enjoyment of His Presence, He would as much cease to act according to the nature of things as if He should punish a being that lived in innocence, for to punish innocence and to reward sin are equally contrary to the nature and reason of things.

I have just mentioned these things to help us to conceive rightly what is meant by the reasonableness and necessity of those tempers which religion requires. As I hope this is sufficient to give anyone a positive assurance that religion is so far from being an imposition upon us, consisting of needless duties, that it is founded in the nature and reason of things, and is as necessary to restore us to the enjoyment of God as it is necessary that God should love things according as they are lovely.

For let anyone carefully consider this proposition, whether it be not absolutely certain that God loveth all things according as they are lovely. Is not this as certain as that God is Reason itself? Could He be infinitely reasonable, or Reason in Perfection, if He did not regard things according to their natures? hating only those things which are truly hateful, and loving things so far as they are lovely? To act by any other rule than the reason and nature of things is to act by humour and caprice. Let this therefore teach us that as we are in ourselves, so we are necessarily either odious or acceptable to God.

This is what I would have understood by the reasonableness of all religious duties and tempers. They are all required because they are as suitable to the reason and nature of things as it is suitable to the reason of things to be thankful for mercies, or fear things that are truly dreadful. Thus, for instance, Humility is nothing else but a right judgment of ourselves, and is only so far enjoined as it is suitable to the truth of our state; for to think worse of ourselves than we really are is no more a virtue than to take five to be less than four. On the contrary, he that is proud offends as much against truth and reason, and judges as falsely of himself, as the madman who fancies himself to be a King, and the straw to which he is chained to be a throne of state. Having observed this much concerning the reasonableness of tempers or duties, which religion demands, I proceed now to show wherein the reasonableness and necessity of self-denial consists.

If a person was to walk upon a rope across some great river, and he was bid to deny himself the pleasure of walking in silver shoes, or looking about at the beauty of the waves, or listening to the noise of sailors, if he was commanded to deny himself the advantage of fishing by the way, would there be any hardship in such self-denial? Would not such self-denials be as reasonable, as commanding him to love things that will do him good, or to avoid things that are hurtful?

Strait is the Gate and narrow is the Way that leadeth unto Life, saith our blessed Saviour. Now if Christians are to walk in *a narrow Way that leadeth to Eternal Life,* the chief business of a Christian must be to deny himself all those things which may either stop or lead him out of his narrow way. And if they think that pleasures and indulgences are consistent with their keeping the narrow way, they think as reasonably as if the man upon the rope should think that he might safely use silver shoes, or stop in his way to catch fish.

For since our souls are in a state of corruption, and our life is a state of probation, in order to alter and remove this corruption, it is certain that every thing and every way of life which nourishes and increases our corruption is as much to be avoided as those things which beget us purity and holiness are to be sought after.

Now Fasting, as it is a denial of bodily indulgences, as it disciplines the body into a state of obedience and contradicts its appetites, is the most constant and universal means of procuring liberty and freedom of mind. For it is the love of our body, and too much care of its enjoyments, that makes us too sensible of its demands, and subject to its tempers. Whatever we nourish and cherish, so far gains an interest in us and rules us in the same degree that it has got our affections. Till therefore religion has entered us into a state of Self-denial, we live in a state that supports the slavery and corruption of our natures. For every indulgence of the body in eating and drinking is adding to its power, and making all our ways of thinking subservient to it.

A man that makes every day a day of full and cheerful meals will by degrees make the happiness of every day depend upon it, and consider everything with regard to it. He will go to Church or stay at home as it suits with his dinner, and not scruple to tell you that he generally eats too heartily to go to the Afternoon Service. Now such people are under a worse disorder of body than he who has the jaundice, and have their judgment more perverted than he who sees all things yellow. For how can they be said to perceive the difference of things who have more taste for the preparations of the kitchen than for the joys and comforts of the House of God, who choose rather to make themselves unfit for Divine Service than to balk the pleasure of a full meal? And this not by chance, or upon some unusual occasion, but by a constant intended course of life.

Let such people deal faithfully with themselves, and search out their spirit. Can they think that they are *born again of God*, that they have the *Spirit of Christ*, who are thus subject to the pleasures of gluttony. Can they be said to treat their bodies as *Temples of the Holy Ghost* who make them unfit for the holy service of public worship? Can they be said to offer their bodies unto God as *a reasonable, holy and living sacrifice?* Can they be said to *love God with all their heart and all their Soul*, or to have *forsaken all* to follow Christ, who will not so much as forsake half a meal for the sake of Divine Worship?

I know it will be thought too severe that I have called this gluttony, because it is the practice of numbers of people of worth and reputation, but I hope they will turn their dislike of the name into a dislike of the thing, for it is as certainly gluttony as picking of pockets is stealing.

If we were to fast without praying, would not this be a way of worship of our own invention? And if we pray and neglect fasting, is it not equally choosing a worship of our own? For he that has taught us the use and advantage of prayer has in the same words taught us the same things of fasting, and has also joined them together as having the same power with God. So that it is as necessary that our lives be a state of regimen, that we live by such rules as are contrary to this variety of disorders, as it is necessary for a man under a complication of habitual distempers to enter into a course of regularity.

I suppose it will be readily granted that all tempers are increased by indulgence, and that the more we yield to any disposition, the stronger it grows. It is therefore certain that self-denial is our only cure, and that we must practise as many sorts of self-denial as we have ill tempers to contend with.

Pride, Hypocrisy, Vanity, Hatred and Detraction are all disorderly indulgences, and have their only cure in Self-denial, as certainly as drunkenness and sensuality. To deny one's self all indulgences of pride and vanity, all instances of falseness and hypocrisy, of envy and spite requires greater care and watchfulness, and a more continual Self-denial than to avoid the motives to intemperance.

And he who thinks to render himself humble any other way than by denying himself all instances of pride is as absurd as he who intends to be sober without abstaining from all degrees of intemperance. For Humility as truly consists in the practice of things that are humble as Justice consists in the doing things that are just. Every virtue is but a mere name, an empty sound till it shows itself by an abstinence from all indulgences of the contrary vice, till it is founded in this self-denial. We are certainly under habits of pride till we are governed by Humility, and we are not governed by Humility till we deny ourselves and are afraid of every appearance of pride, till we are willing to comply with every thing and every state that may preserve and secure our Humility. No man is governed by a religious justice till he is exact in all degrees of it, till he denies himself all approaches towards injustice, till he fears and abhors every appearance of fraud and crafty management.

Now it is this state and temper of mind that is the measure of every virtue.

I have been the longer upon this subject, trying every way to represent the weakness and corruption of our nature because so far as we rightly understand it, so far we see into the reasonableness and necessity of all religious duties. If we fancy ourselves to be wise and regular in our tempers and judgments, we can see no reason for denying ourselves, but if we find that our whole nature is disorder, that our light is darkness, our wisdom foolishness, that our tempers and judgments are as gross and blind as our appetites, that our senses govern children, that our ambition and greatness is taken up with gewgaws and trifles, that the state of our bodies is a state of error and delusion, like that of drunkenness and passion. If we see ourselves in this true light, we shall see the whole reason of Christian self-denial, of meekness and poverty of spirit, of putting off our old man, of renouncing our whole selves that we may see all things in God; of watching and prayer and mortifying all our inclinations, that our hearts may be moved by a motion from God, and our wills and inclinations be directed by the Light and Wisdom of Religion.

Religion has little or no hold of us till we have these right apprehensions of ourselves. It may serve for a little decency of outward behaviour, but it is not the religion of our hearts, till we feel the weakness and disorder of our nature, and embrace piety and devotion as the means of recovering us to a state of Perfection and happiness in God.

VI

OF THE NECESSITY OF DIVINE GRACE AND THE SEVERAL DUTIES TO WHICH IT CALLETH ALL CHRISTIANS

I come now to another Article of our religion, namely, the absolute necessity of Divine Grace, which is another universal and constant reason of Self-denial. The invisible operation and assistance of God's Holy Spirit by which we are disposed towards that which is good, and made able to perform it as a confessed doctrine of Christianity.

Our natural life is preserved by some union with God who is the Fountain of Life to all the creation, to which union we are altogether strangers. We find that we are alive as we find that we think, but how, or by what influence from God our life is supported is a secret into which we cannot enter. It is the same thing with relation to our spiritual life, or Life of Grace, it arises from some invisible union with God, or Divine influence, which in this state of life we cannot comprehend.

Our blessed Saviour saith *The Wind bloweth where it listeth, and thou hearest the sound thereof, but cannot tell whence it cometh and whither it goeth; so is everyone that is born of God.* This shows us how ignorant we are of the manner of the operations of the Holy Spirit. We may feel its effects, as we may perceive the effects of the wind, but are as much strangers to its manner of coming upon us, as we are strangers to that exact point from whence the wind begins to blow, and where it will cease.

The Spirit of God is like the nature of God, too high for our conceptions whilst we are in these dark houses of clay. But our blessed Saviour has in some degree helped our conceptions in this matter by the manner of His giving the Holy Spirit to his disciples. *And he breathed on them, and said unto them, Receive the Holy Ghost.* Now by this ceremony of breathing we are taught to conceive of the communications of the Holy Spirit with some likeness to breath, or wind, that its influences come upon us in some manner most like to a gentle breathing of the air. Representations of this kind are only made in compliance with the weakness of our apprehensions, which not being able to conceive things as they are in their own nature, must be instructed by comparing them to such things as our senses are acquainted with. Thus, the wisdom and knowledge that is revealed from God is compared to light, not because light is a true representation of the wisdom of God, but because it serves best to represent it to our low capacities. In like manner, the influences of the Holy Spirit are set forth by the ceremony of breathing upon us, not because breath, or air, or wind are true representations of the gifts of the Spirit, but because they are the properest representations that yet fall within our knowledge.

But that which is most necessary for us to know, and of which we are sufficiently informed in Scripture is the absolute necessity of this Divine assistance.

The heathen philosophers exhorted man to reverence his reason as a ray of the Deity; but we can go much higher. We can exhort him to reverence the Deity that dwelleth in him, and to act with such purity as becomes persons who are inspired by the Holy Ghost. This is the improvement we are to make of this doctrine of Divine grace. It must make us exact and careful of our behaviour, that we may walk worthy of that Holy Spirit that dwelleth in us.

VII

CHRISTIANS ARE CALLED TO A CONSTANT STATE OF PRAYER AND DEVOTION

It is one principle Article of our Religion to believe that our blessed Saviour is now at the right hand of God, there making perpetual intercession for us till the redemption of mankind is finished. Prayer therefore is undoubtedly a proper means of drawing near to God, a necessary method of restoring sinners to His favour, since He who has conquered sin and death, who is constituted Lord of all is yet, as the great Advocate for sinners, obliged to make perpetual intercession for them.

Whenever, therefore, we are in the spirit of prayer, when our hearts are lifted up to God, breathing out holy petitions to the Throne of Grace, we have this encouragement to be constant and fervent in it, that we are then joining with an intercession at the right hand of God, and doing that for ourselves on earth which our Blessed Saviour is perpetually doing in Heaven. This reason of prayer is perhaps not much considered, yet it certainly contains a most powerful motive to it. For who that considers his redemption as now carrying on by an intercession in Heaven, can think himself so agreeable to God, so like his Saviour, as when the constancy of his own prayers bears some resemblance to that never-ceasing intercession which is made above?

This shows us also that we are most of all to desire those prayers which are offered up at the Altar, where the Body and Blood of Christ are joined with them. For as our prayers are only acceptable to God through the merits of Jesus Christ, so we may be sure that we are praying to God in the most prevailing way when we thus pray in the Name of Christ, and plead His merits in the highest manner that we can.

Devotion may be considered either as an exercise of public or private prayers at set times and occasions, or as a temper of the mind, a state and disposition of the heart, which is rightly affected with such exercises. Now external acts of devotion are like other external actions, very liable to falseness, and are only so far good and valuable as they proceed from a right disposition of heart and mind. Zealous professions of friendship are but the more abominable hypocrisy for being often repeated, unless there be an equal zeal in the heart. So solemn prayers, rapturous devotions, are but repeated hypocrisies unless the heart and mind be conformable to them. Since, therefore, it is the heart only that is devout, since the regularity and fervency of the heart is the regularity and fervency of devotion, I shall consider devotion chiefly in this respect, as it is a state and temper of the heart. For it is in this sense only that Christians are called to a constant state of devotion, they are not to be always on their knees in acts of prayer, but they are to be always in the state and temper of devotion.

Friendship does not require us to be always waiting upon our friends in external services, these offices have their times and seasons of intermission. It is only the service of the heart, the friendship of the mind that is never to intermit. It is not to begin and end, as external services do, but is to persevere in a constancy like the motion of our heart, or the beating of our pulse. It is just so in devotion. Prayers have their hours, their beginning and ending, but that turn of mind, that disposition of the heart towards God which is the life and spirit of prayer is to be as constant and lasting as our own life and spirit. The repeating of a Creed at certain times is an act of faith which overcometh the world, stays neither for times nor seasons, but is a

living principle of the soul, that is always believing, trusting
and depending upon God. In the same manner, verbal
prayers are acts of devotion, but that prayer which saveth,
which openeth the Gates of Heaven, stops not at forms and
manuals of devotion, but is a language of the soul, a judgment of the heart, which worships, adores and delights in
God at all times and seasons.

Let us now put these things together.

It is certain that devotion, as a temper of the mind,
must have something to produce it, as all other tempers
have; that it cannot be taken up at times and occasions,
but must arise from the state of the soul, as all other
tempers and desires do.

It is also equally certain that humility, self-denial and a
renunciation of the world are the only foundation of
devotion, that it can only proceed from these, as from its
proper causes. Here, therefore, we must fix our rule to
take the just measure of ourselves. We must not consider
how many Books of Devotion we have, how often we go
to Church, or how often we have felt a warmth and fervour
in our prayers. These are uncertain signs. But we must
look to the foundations, and assure ourselves that our
devotion neither is, nor can be, greater than our humility,
self-denial and renunciation of the world. For as it must
proceed only from these causes, so it can rise no higher
than they carry it, and must be in the same state of strength
or weakness that they are. If our humility is false, our self-
denial hypocritical and trifling, and our worldly tempers
not half mortified, our devotion will be just in the same
state of falseness, hypocrisy and imperfection. The care
therefore of our devotion seems wholly to consist in the
care of these duties. So far as we proceed in them, so
far we advance in devotion. We must alter our lives in
order to alter our hearts, for it is impossible to live one
way and pray another.

Let me now only add this one word more, that he who

has learned to pray has learned the greatest secret of a holy and happy life.

Which way soever else we let loose our hearts, they will return unto us again empty and weary. Time will convince the vainest and blindest minds that happiness is no more to be found in the things of this world than it is to be dug out of the earth. But when the motions of our hearts are motions of piety, tending to God in constant acts of devotion, love and desire, then have we found rest unto our souls, then is it that we have conquered the misery of our nature, and neither love nor desire in vain; then is it that we have found out a good suited to our natures, that is equal to all our wants, that is a constant source of comfort and refreshment, that will fill us with peace and joyful expectations here, and eternal happiness hereafter. For he that lives in the spirit and temper of devotion, whose heart is always full of God, lives at the top of human happiness, and is the furthest removed from all the vanities and vexations which disturb and weary the minds of men who are devoted to the world.

Since, therefore, it is the great end of our religion to make us fellow-heirs with Christ, and partakers of the same happiness, it is not to be wondered at that our religion should require us to be like Christ in this life, to imitate His example, that we may enter into that state of happiness which He enjoys in the Kingdom of Heaven.

For who can find the least shadow of a reason why he should not imitate the life of Christ, or why Christians should think of any other Rule of Life? It would be as easy to show that Christ acted amiss, as that we need not act after His example. And to think that these are degrees of holiness, which though very good in themselves, are yet not necessary for us to aspire after is the same absurdity as to think that it was not necessary for our Saviour to have been so perfect himself as He was. For give but the reason why such degrees of holiness and purity became our

Saviour, and you will give as good a reason for us to aspire after them. For as the Blessed Jesus took not on Him the nature of Angels, but the nature of Man, as He was in all points made like unto us, sin only excepted, so we are sure that there was no spirit or temper that was excellent in Him that recommended Him to God, but would be also excellent in us and recommend us to God, if we could arrive at it.

There is no falseness of our hearts that leads us into greater errors than imagining that we shall some time or other be better than we are, or need be now; for Perfection has no dependence upon external circumstances, it wants no times or opportunities, but it is then in its highest state when we are making the best use of that condition in which we are placed. Let us therefore not vainly say that if we had lived in our Saviour's days, we would have followed Him, or that if we could work miracles, we would devote ourselves to His glory. For to follow Christ as far as we can in our present state, and to do all that we are able for His glory, is as acceptable to Him as if we were working miracles in His Name.

The greatness that we are to aim at is not the greatness of our Saviour's particular actions, but it is the greatness of His spirit and temper that we are to act by in all parts of our life. For the Blessed Jesus has called us to live as He did, to walk in the same Spirit that He walked, that we may be in the same happiness with Him when this life is at an end. And indeed who can think that anything but the same life can lead to the same state?

VIII

AN EXHORTATION TO CHRISTIAN PERFECTION

WHOEVER hath read the foregoing chapters with attention is, I hope, sufficiently instructed in the knowledge of Christian Perfection. He hath seen that it requireth us to devote ourselves wholly unto God, to make the ends and designs of religion the ends and designs of all our actions. That it calleth us to be born again of God, to live by the light of His Holy Spirit, to renounce the world, and all worldly tempers, to practise a constant, universal self-denial, to make daily wars with the corruption and disorder of our nature, to prepare ourselves for divine grace by a purity and holiness of conversation, to avoid all pleasures and cares which grieve the Holy Spirit and separate Him from us, to live in a daily constant state of prayer and devotion, and as the crown of all to imitate the life and spirit of the Holy Jesus.

I have all along shown that Christian Perfection consists in the right performance of our necessary duties, that it implies such holy tempers as constitute that common piety which is necessary to salvation, and consequently it is such a piety as is equally necessary to be attained by all people. But besides this, we are to consider that God only knows what abatements of holiness He will accept, and therefore we can have no security of our salvation but by doing our utmost to deserve it.

There are different degrees of holiness which it may please God to reward, but we cannot state these different degrees ourselves, but must all labour to be as eminent as we can, and then our different improvements must be left to God. We have nothing to trust to but the sincerity of our endeavours, and our endeavours may well be thought to want sincerity unless they are endeavours after the utmost Perfection. As soon as we stop at any degrees of goodness, we put an end to our goodness, which is only valuable by having all the degrees that we can add to it.

Our highest improvement is a state of great imperfection, but will be accepted by God because it is our highest improvement. But any other state of life where we are not doing all we can to purify and perfect our souls is a state that can give us no comfort or satisfaction, because so far as we are wanting in any ways of piety that are in our power, so far as we are defective in any holy tempers of which we are capable, so far we make our very salvation uncertain. For no one can have any assurance that he pleases God, or puts himself within the terms of Christian salvation, but he who serves God with his whole heart, and with the utmost of his strength. For though the Christian religion be a covenant of mercy for the pardon and salvation of frail and imperfect creatures, yet we cannot say that we are within the conditions of that mercy till we do all that we can in our frail and imperfect state. So that though we are not called to such a Perfection as implies a sinless state, though our imperfections will not prevent the divine mercy, yet it cannot be proved that God has any terms of favour for those who do not labour to be as perfect as they can be.

If you would now devote yourself to Perfection perhaps you must part with some friends, you must displease some relations, you must lay aside some designs, you must refrain from some pleasures, you must alter your life, nay perhaps you must do more than this, you must expose yourself to the hatred of your friends, to the jest and ridicule of wits, and to the scorn and derision of worldly men: but had you not better do and suffer all this than to die less perfect, less prepared for mansions of eternal glory? But indeed the suffering of all this is suffering nothing. For why should it signify anything to you what fools and madmen think of you? And surely it can be no wrong or rash judgment to think those both fools and mad who condemn what God approves, and like that which God condemns. But if you think this too much to be done, to obtain eternal glory, think, on the other hand, what can be gained instead of it.

You would perhaps devote yourself to Perfection, but for this or that little difficulty that lies in your way. You are not in so convenient a state for the full practice of piety as you could wish. But consider that this is nonsense, because Perfection consists in conquering difficulties. You could not be perfect as the present state of trial requires had you not those difficulties and inconveniences to struggle with. These things, therefore, which you would have removed, are laid in your way that you may make them so many steps to Perfection and glory.

Be but your own true friend, and then you have nothing to fear from your enemies. Do you but sincerely labour in the Lord and then neither height nor depth, neither life nor death, neither men nor devils, can make your labour in vain.

AN APPEAL TO ALL THAT DOUBT OR DISBELIEVE THE TRUTHS OF THE GOSPEL WHETHER THEY BE DEISTS, ARIANS, SOCINIANS, OR NOMINAL CHRISTIANS

In which the True Grounds and Reasons of the Whole Christian Faith and Life are Plainly and Fully Demonstrated.

By WILLIAM LAW, M.A.

(Abridged)

THE CONTENTS

I

Of Creation in general. Of the Origin of the Soul. Whence
Will and Thought are in the Creature. Why the Will is
Free. The Origin of Evil solely from the Creature. This
World not a first, immediate Creation of God. How the
World comes to be in this present State. The first Per-
fection of Man. All Things prove a Trinity in God. Man
hath the triune Nature of God in Him. Arianism and
Deism confuted by Nature. That Life is uniform through
all Creatures. That there is but one kind of Death to be
found in all Nature. The fallen Soul hath the Nature of
Hell in it. Regeneration is a real Birth of a Divine Life in
the Soul. That there is but one Salvation possible in
Nature. This Salvation only to be had from Jesus Christ.
All the Deist's Faith and Hope proved to be false. 73

II

Of External and Temporal Nature. How Nature is from
God, and the Scene of His Action. How the Creatures
are out of it. Temporal Nature created out of that which
is eternal. The fallen Angels brought the first Disorders
into Nature. This World created to repair those Disorders. Whence Good and Evil is in every Thing of this
World. How Heaven and Hell make up the Whole of
this World. How the Fire of this World differs from
eternal Fire; and the Matter of this World from the
Materiality of Heaven. Eternal Nature is the Kingdom of
Heaven, the beatific Manifestation of the triune God.
God is mere Love and Goodness. How Wrath and Anger
come to be ascribed to him. Of Fire in general. Of the
Unbeginning Fire. Of the Spirituality of Fire. How
Fire comes to be in material Things. Whence the

IT HAS been an opinion commonly received, though without any foundation in the light of nature, or Scripture, that God created this whole visible world and all things in it out of nothing. Nay, that the souls of men, and the highest orders of beings were created in the same manner. The Scripture is very decisive against this original of the souls of men. For Moses saith, *'God breathed into man'* (*Spiraculum Vitarum*) *the Breath of Lives, and man 'became a living soul.'* Here the notion of a soul created out of nothing is in the plainest, strongest manner rejected by the first written Word of God, and no Jew or Christian can have the least excuse for falling into such an error. Here the highest and most divine original is not darkly, but openly, absolutely and in the strongest form of expression ascribed to the soul. It came forth as a Breath of Life, or Lives, out from the mouth of God, and therefore did not come out of the womb of nothing, but is what it is, and has what it has in itself, from and out of the first and highest of all Beings.

But the incontestable ground or reason of an immortal life and eternal relation between God and the whole human nature, and which lays all mankind under the same obligations to the same true worship of God, is most fully set forth by Moses, who alone tells us the true fact: how and why man is immortal in his nature, *viz.* because the beginning of his life was a Breath breathed into him by God, and for this end, that he might be a living image and likeness of God, created to partake of the nature and immortality of God. This is the great doctrine of the Jewish legislator, and which justly places him amongst the greatest preachers of true religion. St. Paul used a very powerful argument to persuade the Athenians to own the true God and the true religion when he told them *'that God made the world and all things therein, that He giveth Life and Breath and all Things; that He hath made of one Blood all nations of men to dwell on the earth; that they should all seek the Lord, if haply they might feel after and find him, seeing He is not far from any of us because in Him we live, move and have our being.'*

And yet this doctrine, which St. Paul preaches to the Athenians, is nothing else but that same divine and heavenly instruction which he had learnt from Moses, which Moses openly and plainly taught all the Jews. The Jewish theocracy therefore was by no means an intimation to that people that they had no concern with the true God, but as children of this world, under His temporal protection or punishment, for their lawgiver left them no room for such a thought, because he had as plainly taught them their eternal nature and eternal relation which they had to God in common with all mankind, as St. Paul did to the Athenians, who only set before them that very doctrine that Moses taught all the Jews. The great end of the Jewish theocracy was to show, both to Jew and Gentile, the absolute uncontrollable power of the one God by such a convenanted interposition of His providence that all the world might know that the one God from whom both Jew and Gentile were fallen away by departing from the faith and religion of their first fathers, was the only God from whom all mankind could receive either blessing or cursing.

Herein also appears the high dignity and never-ceasing perpetuity of our nature. The essences of our souls can never cease to be because they never began to be, and nothing can live eternally but that which hath lived from all Eternity.

The essences of our soul were a breath in God before they became a living soul, they lived in God before they

lived in the created soul, and therefore the soul is a partaker of the eternity of God and can never cease to be.
Here, O Man, behold the great original and the high state
of thy birth. Here let all that is within thee praise thy
God who has brought thee into so high a state of being,
who has given thee powers as eternal and boundless as His
own attributes, that there might be no end or limits of
thy happiness in Him. Thou begannest as time began, but
as time was in eternity before it became days and years, so
thou wast in God before thou wast brought into the
Creation. And as time is neither a part of eternity, nor
broken off from it, yet come out of it, so thou art not a
part of God, nor broken off from Him, yet born out of
Him.

To suppose a willing, understanding being created out
of nothing is a great absurdity. For as thinking and willing
must have always been from all eternity, or they could
never have been either in eternity or time, so wherever
they are found in any particular finite beings, must of
all necessity be direct communications, or propagations
of that thinking and willing which never could begin to be.
The creation, therefore, of a soul is not the creation of
thinking and willing, or the making that to be and to think
which before had nothing of being or thought, but it is the
bringing the powers of thinking and willing out of their
eternal state in the One God into a beginning state of a
self-conscious life, distinct from God. And this is God's
omnipotent, creating ability that He can make the powers
of His own nature become creatural, living, personal
images of what He is in Himself, in a state of distinct
personality from Him, so that the creature is one in its
limited, finite state, as God is one, and yet hath nothing in
it but that which was in God before it came into it.

For the creature, be it what it will, high or low, can be
nothing else but a limited participation of the nature of the
Creator. Nothing can be in the creature but what came

from the Creator, and the Creator can give nothing to the creature but that which it hath in itself to give. And if beings could be created out of nothing, the whole creation could be no more a proof of the being of God than if it had sprung up itself out of nothing. For if they are brought into being out of nothing, then they can have nothing of God in them, and so can bear no testimony of God, but are as good a proof that there is no God, as that there is one. But if they have any Thing of God in them, then they cannot be said to be created out of nothing.

That the souls of men were not created out of nothing, but are born out of an Eternal Original is plain from hence; from that delight in and desire of eternal existence which is so strong and natural to the soul of man. For nothing can delight in, or desire eternity, or so much as form a notion of it, or think upon it, or in any way reach after it, but that alone which is generated from it and come out of it.

Again. Every soul shrinks back and is frightened at the very thought of falling into nothing. Now this undeniably proves that the soul was not created out of nothing. For it is an eternal truth, spoken by all nature, that every thing strongly aspires after, and cannot be easy, till it finds and enjoys the Original out of which it arose. If the soul, therefore, was brought out of nothing, all its being would be a burden to it. It would want to be dissolved, and to be delivered from every kind and degree of sensibility, and nothing could be so sweet and agreeable to it as to think of falling back into that nothingness out of which it was called forth by its creation.

If the soul was not born or created out of God, it could have no happiness in God, no desire, nor any possibility of enjoying Him. If it had nothing of God in it, it must stand in the utmost distance of contrariety to Him, and be utterly incapable of living, moving and having its being in God. For every thing must have the nature of that out of which it was created, and must live and have its being in that Root or Ground from whence it sprung. If, therefore, there was nothing of God in the soul, nothing that is in God could do the soul any good, or have any kind of communication with it, but the gulf of separation between God and the soul would be even greater than that which is between Heaven and Hell.

But let us rejoice that our soul is a thinking, willing, understanding being, full of thoughts, cares, longings and desires of eternity, for this is our full proof that our descent is from God Himself, that we are born out of Him, breathed forth from Him; that our soul is of an eternal nature, made a thinking, willing understanding creature out of that which hath willed and thought in God from all eternity, and therefore must be, for ever and ever, a partaker of the eternity of God.

And here you may behold the sure Ground of the absolute impossibility of the annihilation of the Soul. Its essences never began to be, and therefore can never cease to be. They had an eternal reality before they were in, or became a distinct soul, and therefore they must have the same eternal reality in it. It was the Eternal Breath of God before it came into man, and therefore the eternity of God must be inseparable from it. It is no more a property of the Divine Omnipotence to be able to annihilate a soul than to be able to make an eternal truth become a fiction of yesterday; and to think it a lessening of the power of God to say that He cannot annihilate the soul is as absurd as to say that it is a lessening of the light of the sun if it cannot destroy or darken its own rays of light.

It is impossible that this world, in the state and condition it is now in, should have been an immediate and original creation of God. This is as impossible as that God should create evil, either natural or moral. Therefore it is as impossible that this outward state and condition of things should be a first and immediate work of God, as that there should be good and evil in God Himself. All storms and tempests, every fierceness of heat, every wrath of cold proves with the same certainty that outward nature is not a first work of God, as the selfishness, envy, pride, wrath and malice of Devils and men proves that they are not in the first state of their creation. Thus all that is on earth is only a change or alteration of something that was in Heaven. And Heaven itself is nothing else but the first glorious out-birth, the majestic manifestation, the beatific visibility of the One God in Trinity. And thus we find out how this temporal nature is related to God. It is only a gross out-birth of that which is an eternal nature, or a blessed Heaven, and stands only in such degree of distance from it as water does to air, and this is the reason why the last fire will and must turn this gross temporal nature into its first heavenly state.

But to suppose the gross matter of this world to be made out of nothing, or to be a grossness that has proceeded from nothing, or compacted nothing, is more absurd than to suppose ice that has congealed nothing, a yard that is not made up of inches, or a pound that is not the product of ounces.

All the qualities of all beings are eternal. No real equality or power can appear in any creature but what has its eternal root, or generating cause in the creator. If a quality could begin to be in a creature which did not always exist in the Creator, it would be no absurdity to say that a thing might begin to be without any cause either of its beginning or being.

All qualities, properties, or whatever can be affirmed of God, are self-existent, and necessary existent. Self and necessary existence is not a particular attribute of God, but is the general nature of every thing that can be affirmed of God. All qualities and properties are self-existent in God. Now, they cannot change their nature when they are derived, or formed into creatures, but must have the same self-birth, and necessary existence in the creature which they had in the Creator. The creature begins to be, when and as it pleased God, but the qualities which are become creaturely, and which constitute the creature are self-existent, just as the same qualities are in God. Thus, thinking, willing and desire can have no outward Maker, their Maker is in themselves, they are self-existent powers wherever they are, whether in God or in the creature, and as they form themselves in God, so they form themselves in the creature. But now if no quality can begin to be, if all the qualities and powers of creatures must be eternal and necessary existent in God, before they can have any existence in any creature, then it undeniably follows that every created thing must have its whole nature from, and out of the Divine Nature.

All qualities are not only good, but infinitely perfect, as they are in God, and it is absolutely impossible that they should have any evil or defect in them as they are in the One God, who is the great and universal All. Because, where all properties are, there must necessarily be an all possible Perfection, and that which must always have All in itself must, by an absolute necessity, be always all perfect. But the same qualities thus infinitely good and perfect in God become imperfect and evil in the creature, because in the creature, being limited and finite, they may be divided and separated from one another by the creature itself.

Thus strength and fire in the Divine Nature are nothing else but the strength and flame of Love, and never can be anything else; but in the creature, strength and fire may be separated from Love, and then they are become an evil, they are wrath and darkness and all mischief. And thus that same strength and quality which in creatures making a right use of their own will and self-motion becomes their goodness and Perfection, doth in creatures making a wrong use of their will become their evil and mischievous nature. And it is a truth that deserves well to be considered, that there is no goodness in any creature, from the highest to the lowest, but in its continuing to be in such an union of qualities and powers as God has brought together in its creation.

In the highest order of created beings, this is their standing in their first Perfection, this is their fulfilling the whole Will or Law of God, this is their piety, their song of praise, their eternal adoration of their great Creator.

On the other hand, there is no evil, no guilt, no deformity in any creature but in its dividing and separating itself from something which God had given to be in union with it. This, and this alone, is the whole nature of all good and all evil in the creature, both in the moral and natural world, in spiritual and material things. For instance, dark fiery wrath in the soul is not only very like, but it is the very self-same thing in the soul which a wrathful poison is in the flesh. Now, the qualities of poison are in themselves good qualities, and necessary to every life; but they are become a poisonous evil because they are separated from some other qualities. Thus also the qualities of fire and strength that constitute an evil wrath in the soul, are in themselves very good qualities, and necessary to every good life, but they are become an evil wrath because separated from some other qualities with which they should be united.

The qualities of the Devil and all fallen Angels are good qualities; they are the very same which they received from their infinitely perfect Creator, the very same which are, and must be in all heavenly Angels, but they are an hellish, abominable malignity in them now because they have, by their own self-motion, separated them from the light and love which should have kept them glorious Angels.

And here may be seen at once, in the clearest light, the true origin of all evil in the creation without the least imputation upon the Creator. God could not possibly create a creature to be an infinite All, like Himself; God could not bring any creature into existence but by deriving into it the self-existent, self-generating, self-moving qualities of His own nature. For the qualities must be in the creature that which they were in the Creator, only in a state of limitation, and therefore every creature must be finite, and must have a self-motion, and so must be capable of moving right and wrong, of uniting or dividing from what it will, or of falling from that state in which it ought to stand.

But as every quality in every creature, both within and without itself, is equally good, and equally necessary to the Perfection of the creature, since there is nothing that is evil in it, nor can become evil to the creature but from itself, by its separating That from itself with which it can and ought to be united, it plainly follows that evil can no more be charged upon God, than darkness can be charged upon the sun, because every quality is equally good, every quality of fire is as good as every quality of light and only becomes an evil to that creature who, by his own self-motion, has separated fire from the light in his own nature. And thus you see the uniform Life of all the Creatures of God. How they are all raised, enriched and blessed by the same life of God, derived into different kingdoms of creatures. For the beginnings of progress of a perfect life in fruits, for the beginnings and progress of a perfect life in Angels are not like to one another, but are the very same thing, or the working of the very same qualities only in different kingdoms.

Astringency in a fruit is the same quality and does the same work in a fruit that attracting desire does in a spiritual being. It is the same beginner, former and supporter of a creaturely life in the one as in the other. No creature in Heaven or earth can begin to be but by this astringency or desire being made the ground of it. And yet this astringency, kept from the virtue of the sun can only produce a poisonous fruit, and this astringent desire in an Angel, turned from the light of God, can only make a Devil. The biting, stinging bitterness of a fruit, if you could add thought to it, would be the very gnawing envy of the Devil. And the envious motion in the Devil's nature would be nothing else but that stinging bitterness which is in a fruit if you could take thought from the Devil's motion.

That there is an attracting desire in the Divine Nature is undeniable because attraction is essential to all bodies, and desire, which is the same quality, is absolutely inseparable from all intelligible beings. Therefore that which is necessarily existent in the creature upon the supposition of its creation, must necessarily be in the Creator, because no inherent operative quality can be in the creature unless the same kind of quality has been in the Creator. Therefore, attraction or desire, which are inseparable from every created being and life, are only various participations of the Divine desire, or emanations from it, formed into different kingdoms of Creatures, and working in all of them according to their respective natures. In vegetables, it is that attraction or desire which brings every growing thing to its highest Perfection. In Angels it is that blessed hunger by which they are filled with the Divine nature. In Devils, it is turned into that serpentine selfishness, or crooked desire which makes them a hell and torment to themselves.

On the other hand, as we thus prove *a posteriori* from a view of the creature that there must be an attracting desire in the Divine nature, so we can prove *a priori* also from a consideration of God, that there must be an attracting desire in every thing that ever was, or can be created by God. For nothing can come into being but because God wills and desires it, therefore the desire of God is the Creator, the original of every thing.

The creating will or desire of God is not a distant or separate thing, as when a man wills or desires something to be done or removed at a distance from him, but it is an omnipresent working will and desire which is itself the beginning and forming of the thing desired. Our own will and desirous imagination when they work and create in us a settled aversion, or fixed love of anything resemble in some degree the creating power of God which makes things out of itself, or its own working desire. And our will and working imagination could not have the power that it has now even after the Fall, but because it is a product or spark of that first Divine will or desire which is omnipotent.

Will or desire in the Deity is justly considered as God the Father, Who from eternity to eternity, wills or generates only the Son, from which eternal generating the Holy Spirit eternally proceeds. And this is the infinite Perfection or fulness of beatitude of the life of the Triune God. And every created thing in Heaven and earth attains its Perfection by its gaining in some degree the birth of the Son and Holy Spirit of God in it. For all attraction and desire in the creature generates in them as it did in God; and so the birth of the Son and Holy Spirit of God arises in some degree or other in all creatures that are in their proper state of Perfection.

And there lies the ground of that plain and most fundamental doctrine of Scripture, that the Father is the Creator, the Son the Regenerator, and the Holy Spirit the Sanctifier. For what is this but saying in the plainest manner that as there are Three in God, so there must be Three in the creature, that as the Three stand related to one another in God, so must they stand in the same relation in the creature. For if a threefold life of God must have distinct shares in the Creation, Blessing and Perfection of Man, is it not a demonstration that the life of Man must stand in the same threefold state, and have such a Trinity in it as has its true likeness to that Trinity which is in God.

And the reason why this great mystery of a Trinity in the Deity is thus revealed to us, and the necessity of a baptism in the Name of the Father, Son and Holy Spirit laid upon us is this; it is to show us that the Divine Triune Life of God is lost in us, and that nothing less than a birth from the Son and Holy Spirit of God in us can restore us to our first likeness to that Triune God who at first created us. When man was created in his original Perfection, the Holy Trinity was his Creator, the Breath of Lives, which became a living soul, was the Breath of the Triune God. But when man began to will and desire, that is to generate contrary to the Deity, then the life of the Triune God extinguished in him.

The desire of man being turned from God lost the birth of the Son and the proceeding of the Holy Spirit, and so fell into, or under the light and spirit of this world. That is of a Paradisaical Man enjoying union and communion with Father, Son and Holy Ghost, and living on earth in such enjoyment of God as the Angels live in Heaven, he became an earthly creature, subject to the dominion of this outward world, capable of all its evil influences, subject to its vanity and mortality, and as to his outward life, stood only in the highest rank of animals. This and this alone is the true nature and degree of the Fall of Man. It was neither more nor less than this. It was a falling out of one world, or kingdom, into another, it was changing the Life, Light and Spirit of God for the light and spirit of this world.

The Circle of the Birth of Life in every Creature is its necessary Circumference, and it cannot possibly reach any further, and therefore it is a joyful truth that beings created to worship and adore the Holy Trinity, and to enter into the beatific Life and presence of the Triune God must of all necessity have the same triune life in their own creaturely being. When we thus know the Trinity in ourselves, and adore its high original in the Deity, we are possessed of a truth of the greatest moment, that enlightens the mind with the most solid and edifying knowledge, and opens to us the fullest understanding of all that concerns the Creation, Fall and Redemption of Man. Without this knowledge all the Scripture will be used as a dead letter and formed only into figurative, historical system of things that has no ground in nature, and learned Divines can only be learned in the explication of phrases and verbal distinctions. The first chapters of *Genesis* will be a knot that cannot be untied. The mysteries of the Gospel will only be called foederal rites, and their inward ground reproached as enthusiastic dreams, but when it is known that the Triune Nature of God was brought forth in the creation of Man, that it was lost in his Fall, that it is restored in his redemption, a never-failing light arises in all Scripture from *Genesis* to the *Revelation*.

Every thing that is said of God, as Father, Regenerator, or Sanctifier of man; every thing that is said of Jesus Christ as redeeming, forming, dwelling in and quickening; and of the Holy Spirit as moving and sanctifying us; every thing that is said of the Holy Sacraments, or promised in or by them, has its deep and inward ground fully discovered, and the whole Christian religion is built upon a Rock, and that Rock is Nature, and God will appear to be doing every good to us, that the God of all Nature can possibly do.

The doctrine of the Holy Trinity is wholly practical. It is revealed to us to discover our high original, and the greatness of our Fall, to show us the deep and profound operation of the Triune God in the recovery of the Divine Life in our souls, that by the means of this Mystery thus discovered, our piety may be rightly directed, our faith and prayer have their proper objects, that the workings and aspirings of our own hearts may co-operate and correspond with that triune life in the Deity which is always desiring to manifest itself in us.

Now as all creatures, whether intellectual, animate or inanimate, are products or emanations of the Divine Desire, created out of the Father who from eternity to eternity generates the Son, whence the Holy Spirit eternally proceeds; so every intelligent, created being, not fallen from its state, stands in the same birth, or generating desire, it generates in its degree, as God the Father generates eternally the Son, and is blessed and perfected in the Divine Life by having the Holy Spirit arise up in it.

God is all Good, and every thing that comes out from Him as His creature, product or offspring, must come forth in that state of goodness which it had in Him, and every creature, however high in its birth from God, must in the beginning of its life have a power of joining with or departing from God, because the beginning of its life is nothing else but the beginning of its own self-motion as a creature; and therefore no creature can have its state or condition fixed till it gives itself up either wholly unto God, or turns wholly from Him, for if it is an intelligent creature, it can only be so by having the intelligent will of God derived into it, or made creaturely in it; but the intelligent will brought into a creaturely form must be that which it was in its Creator, and therefore must be the same self-existent and self-moving power that it was before it became creaturely in any Angel or Spirit. And thus the cause and origin of evil, wherever it is, is absolutely and eternally separated from God. Now as there is but one God, so there is but one nature, as unalterable as that God from whom it arises, and whose manifestation it is; so also there is but one Religion founded in nature, and but one salvation possible in nature.

Revealed religion is nothing else but a Revelation of the mysteries of Nature, for God cannot reveal or require any thing by a spoken or written word, but that which He reveals and requires by Nature; for Nature is His great Book of Revelation, and he that can only read its capital letters will have found so many demonstrations of the truth of the written Revelation of God.

But to show that there is but one salvation possible in nature, and that possibility solely contained in the Christian method. Look from the top to the bottom of all creatures, from the highest to the lowest beings, and you will find that Death has but one nature in all worlds and in all creatures. Look at life in an Angel and life in a vegetable, and you will find that life has but one and the same form, one and the same ground in the whole scale of beings. No Omnipotence of God can make that to be life which is not life, or that to be death which is not death, according to nature, and the reason is because Nature is nothing else but God's own outward manifestation of what He inwardly is, and can do, and therefore no revelation from God can teach or require any thing but that which is taught and required by God in and through Nature.

The mysteries of Religion, therefore, are no higher nor deeper than the mysteries of Nature, and all the rites, laws, ceremonies, types, institutions and ordinances given by God from Adam to the Apostles, are only typical of something that is to be done, or instrumental to the doing of that which the unchangeable working of Nature requires to be done. As sure therefore as there is but one and the same thing that is Death, and one and the same thing that is Life throughout all Nature, whether temporal or eternal, so sure is it that there is but one way to Life or Salvation for fallen Man. And this Way, let it be what it will, must and can be only that which has its reason and foundation in that one universal Nature which is the one unchangeable manifestation of the Deity.

For if there is but one thing that is Life, and one thing that is Death throughout all Nature, from the highest Angel to the hardest flint upon earth, then it must be plain that the life which is to be raised or restored by religion must and can only be restored according to Nature. And therefore true religion can only be the religion of Nature and Divine Revelation can do nothing else but reveal and manifest the demands and workings of Nature.

Now the one great doctrine of the Christian Religion,

and which includes all the rest, is this, that Adam by his sin died to the Kingdom of Heaven, or that the Divine Life extinguished in him; that he cannot be redeemed or restored to this first Divine Life, but by having it kindled or regenerated in him by the Son and Holy Spirit of God. Now that which is here called Death, his losing the light and spirit of the Kingdom of Heaven, and that which is here made necessary to make him alive again to the Kingdom of Heaven, is that very same which is called and is Death and Life throughout all Nature, both temporal and eternal. And therefore the Christian Religion requiring this method of raising man to a Divine Life has its infallible proof from all Nature.

Again, it is a Scripture doctrine of the utmost certainty and importance that those souls which have totally resisted and withstood all that God has done in them and for them by His Son Jesus Christ, will, at their departure from the body, be incapable of any thing but eternal death, or a hellish condition. Now how can you possibly hold this doctrine of Scripture without holding at the same time that the soul was in that state by the Fall before it had received its Redeemer, as it is then in when it has refused to receive Him, for all that you can say of a lost soul is only this, that it has lost its Redeemer and therefore is only in the condition of that soul which has not received Him. And therefore if a lost soul is only an unredeemed soul it must be plain that the soul, before it had received its Redeemer, was in the miserable condition and had the miserable nature of a lost soul, and therefore the only difference between the fallen soul and the lost soul is this, they are both in the same need of a Saviour, both have the same miserable nature because they have Him not; but the one has the offer of Him, and the other has refused to accept of Him. But his final refusal of Him has only left him in possession of that fallen state of a hellish condition which it had before a Saviour was given to it.

God comes not to judgment to display any wrath of His own, or to inflict any punishment as from Himself upon man. He only comes to declare that all temporary Nature is at an end, and that therefore all things must be, and stand in their own places in eternal Nature. His sentence of condemnation is only a leaving them that are lost in such a misery of their own nature as has finally rejected all that was possible to relieve it.

You fancy that God will not reject you at the last day for having not received this, or that mode or kind of religion, but here all is mistake again. You might as well imagine that no particular kind of element was necessary to extinguish fire, or that water can supply the place of air in kindling it, as suppose that no particular kind of religion is absolutely necessary to raise up such a Divine Life in the soul as can only be its salvation. For Nature is the ground of all creatures, it is God's manifestation of Himself, it is His instrument in and by which He acts in the production and government of every life, and therefore a life that is to belong to this world must be raised according to temporal Nature, and a life that is to live in the next world must be raised according to eternal Nature. Therefore all the particular doctrines, institutions, mysteries and ordinances of a revealed religion that comes from the God of Nature must have their reason, foundation and necessity in Nature; and then your renouncing such a revealed religion is renouncing *all* that the God of Nature can do to save you.

And now, my dear Friend, beware of prejudice, or hardness of heart. One careless or one relenting thought upon all that is here laid before you may either quite shut out, or quite open an entrance for true conviction. I have shown you what is meant by Christian Redemption, and the absolute necessity of a new and heavenly birth in order to obtain your share of a heavenly life in the next world, I have confirmed the truths of the Gospel by proofs taken from what is undeniable in Nature, and I readily grant you that nothing can be true in revealed religion but what has its foundation in Nature, because a religion coming from the God of Nature can have no other end but to reform and set right the failings, transgressions and violations of Nature.

When the Gospel saith that man, fallen from the state of his creation and become an earthly animal of this temporal world, must be born again of the Son and Holy Spirit of God in order to be a heavenly creature, 'tis because all Nature saith that an immortal, eternal soul must have an immortal, eternal Light and Spirit to make it live in Eternal Nature, as every animal must have a temporal light and spirit in order to live in temporary Nature. Must you not therefore either deny the Immortality of the soul or acknowledge the necessity of its having an Eternal Light and Spirit? When the Gospel saith that nothing can kindle or generate the heavenly life but the operation of the Light and Spirit of Heaven, it is because all Nature saith that no temporal life can be raised but in the same manner in temporary Nature. Must you not therefore be forced to confess that Nature and the Gospel both preach the same truths.

God's Goodness or Compassion is always in the same infinite state, always flowing forth, in and through all Nature in the same infinite manner and nothing wants it but that which cannot receive it. Whilst the Angels stood, they stood encompassed with the infinite Source of all goodness and compassion, God was communicated to them in as high a degree as their nature could receive; and they fell, not because He ceased to be an infinite open fountain of all good to them, but because they had a will which must direct itself. For the Will, at its first arising in the creature, can be subject to no outward power because it has no outward maker; as it stands in a creaturely form, God is the true Creator; but as a Will, it has no outward

Maker, but is a ray or spark, derived from the unbeginning Will of the Creator and is of the same nature in the creature as it was in the Creator, self-existent, self-generating, self-moving and uncontrollable from without; and there could not possibly be a free Will in the creature but by its being directly derived or propagated from the same Will in the Creator, for nothing can be free now but that which always was so.

But if the free Will of God, which is above and superior to Nature, be communicated to the creature, then the creature's free Will must have the same power over its one nature that the Will of God has over that eternal nature which is His own manifestation. And therefore every free creature must have and find its own nature in this, or that state, as a birth from the free working of its own will. And here appears the true reason why no creatures of this world can commit sin, 'tis because they have no Will which is superior to Nature. Their Will in every one of them is only the Will of Nature, and therefore let them do what they will, they are always doing that which is *natural* and consequently not *sinful*. But the Will of Angels and Men being an offspring or ray derived from the Will of God, which is superior to Nature, stands chargeable with the state and condition of their nature, and therefore it is that the nature of the Devil, and the nature of fallen Man, is imputed to both of them as their sin, which could not be but because their will was uncontrollable, and gave birth and being to that state and condition of nature which is called and is their sin.

The truth of the matter is this, God is as infinite and boundless in love and goodness as He is in power, but His omnipotence can only do that which is possible, and nothing is possible but that which hath its possibility in Nature. Because Nature is God's first power, His great, universal manifestation of His Deity, in and through and by which all His infinite attributes break forth and display themselves. So that to expect that God should do any thing that is above or contrary to this nature is as absurd as to expect that God should act above, or contrary to Himself.

As God can only make a creature to be in and through and by Nature, so the reason why He cannot make a creature to be and not to be at the same time is only this, because it is contrary to Nature. Let no man therefore trust to be saved at the last Day by an arbitrary goodness, or free grace of God, for salvation is, and can be nothing else, but the having put off all that is damnable and hellish in our nature, which salvation can be found by no creature but by its own full conforming to, and concurring with those mysterious means which the free grace of God hath afforded for the recovery of our first, perfect, glorious state in Nature.

II

EVERY thing that is in being is either God, or Nature, or Creature; and every thing that is not God is only a manifestation of God, for as there is nothing, neither Nature, nor Creature, but what must have its being in, and from God, so every thing is and must be according to its nature, more or less a manifestation of God.

Everything therefore by its form and condition speaks so much of God, and God in every thing speaks and manifests so much of Himself. Temporary Nature is this beginning, created system of sun, stars and elements; 'tis temporary Nature because it begins and hath an end, and is therefore only a temporary manifestation of God, or God manifested according to transitory things. Properly and strictly speaking nothing can begin to be. The beginning of every thing is nothing more than its beginning to be in a new state. Thus Time itself does not begin to be, but duration, which always was, began to be measured by the earth's turning round, or the rising and setting of the sun, and that is called the beginning of time, which is, properly speaking, only the beginning of the measure of duration.

Thus it is with all temporal Nature and all the qualities and powers of temporal beings that live in it. No quality or power of Nature then began to be, but such qualities and powers as had been from all eternity, began then to be in a new state. Ask what Time is, it is nothing else but something of eternal duration become finite, measurable and transitory? Ask what fire, light, darkness, air, water and earth are; they are and can be nothing else but some eternal things become gross, finite, measurable, divisible and transitory? For if there could be a temporal fire that did not spring out of eternal fire, then there might be Time that did not come out of Eternity.

'Tis thus with every temporary thing, and the qualities of it. 'Tis the beginning of nothing, but only of a new state of something that existed before. Therefore all temporary Nature is a product, offspring or out-birth of eternal Nature, and is nothing else but so much of eternal Nature changed from its eternal to a temporary condition.

Now the good and evil that is in this world is that same good and evil and in the same strife that it was in the kingdom of the fallen Angels, only with this happy difference, there it was under the Devil's power, and in a way to be wholly evil; here it is in a new compacted or created state under the providence and blessing of God, appointed to bring forth a new kind of life, and display the wonders of Divine Love, till such time as a new race and angelical creatures born in this mixture of good and evil, shall be fit to receive the Kingdom of Lucifer restored to its first glory. Is there any part of the Christian religion that does not either suppose or speak this great truth, any part of outward Nature that does not confirm it? Is there any part of the Christian religion that is not made more intelligible, more beautiful and edifying by it? Is there any difficulty of outward Nature that is not totally removed and satisfied by it? He that thus knows what this world is, has great reason to be glad that he is born into it, and yet still greater reason to rejoice in being called out of it, preserved from it, and shown how to escape with the preservation of his soul.

O Man! consider thyself, here thou standest in the earnest, perpetual strife of good and evil, all Nature is continually at work to bring about the great Redemption; the whole Creation is travelling in pain and laborious working to be delivered from the vanity of time, and will thou be asleep? Everything thou hearest or seest, says nothing, shows nothing to thee but what either eternal light or eternal darkness hath brought forth, for as day and night divide the whole of our time, so Heaven and Hell divide the whole of our thoughts, word and actions. Stir which way thou wilt, do or design what thou wilt, thou must be an agent with the one or with the other. Thou canst not stand still because thou livest in the perpetual workings of temporal and eternal Nature. If thou workest not with the Good, the evil that is in Nature carries thee along with it. Thou hast the height and depth of eternity in thee, and therefore by doing what thou wilt, either in the closet, the field, the shop or the Church, thou art sowing *That* which grows and must be reaped in eternity. Nothing of thine can vanish away, but every thought, motion and desire of thy heart has its effect either in the height of Heaven or in the depth of Hell. And as time is upon the wing to put an end to the strife of good and evil and bring about the last great separation of all things into their eternal state, with such speed art thou making haste either to be wholly an Angel, or wholly a Devil. O! therefore awake, watch and pray and join with all thy force with that goodness of God which has created time and all things in it to have a happy end in eternity.

All matter in this world is only the materiality of Heaven thus altered. The difference between matter in this world and matter in the other world lies wholly and solely in this: in the one it is *dead*, in the other it is *living* materiality. It is dead materiality in the world because it is gross, dark, hard, heavy, divisible, etc. It is in this state of death because it is separated or broken off from the eternal light, which is the true life, or the power of life in every thing.

That the deadness of the earth may, and certainly will be brought to life by the united power of fire and light is sufficiently shown us by the nature and office of the sun. The sun is the united power of fire and light, and therefore the sun is the raiser of life out of the deadness of the earth, but because fire and light as united in the sun is only the virtue of temporary fire and light, so it can only raise a short and fading transitory life. But as sure as you see that fire and light united in the sun can change the deadness of the earth into such a beautiful variety of a vegetable life, so sure are you that this dark, gross earth is in its state of death and darkness only for this reason, because it is broken off from the united power of fire and light.

For as sure as the outward operation of the fire and light of the sun can change the deadness of the earth into a degree of life, so sure is it that the earth lies in its present darkness because it is separated from its own eternal fire and light. And as sure as you see that the fire and light of the sun can raise a temporal life out of the earth, so sure is it that the united power of eternal fire and light can and will turn all that is earthly into its first state of life and beauty. For the sun of this world, as it is the union of temporal fire and light, has no power, but as it is the outward agent, or temporary representative of eternal fire and light, and therefore it can only do that in part, and imperfectly in time which by the eternal fire and light will be wholly and perfectly done in eternity. And therefore every vegetable life, and every beauty, power and virtue which the sun calls forth out of the earth tells us with a divine certainty that there will come a time when all that is hid in the deadness, grossness and darkness of the earth will be again called up to a perfection of life and glory of beauty.

All beings that are purely of this world have their existence in and dependence upon temporal Nature. God is no Maker, Creator or Governor of any being or creature of this world immediately or by Himself, but He creates, upholds and governs all things of this world by and through and with temporal Nature. As temporary Nature is nothing else but eternal Nature separated, divided, compacted, made visible and changeable for a time, so Heaven is nothing else but the beatific visibility, the majestic preference of the abyssal, unsearchable, Triune God. 'Tis that light with which the Scripture saith God is *decked as with a garment*, and by which He is manifested and made visible to heavenly eyes and beings, for Father, Son and Holy Ghost, as they are the Triune God, deeper than the Kingdom of Heaven or eternal Nature, are invisible to all created eyes, but that beatific visibility and outward glory which is called the Kingdom of Heaven, is the manifestation of the Father, Son and Holy Ghost, in and by and through the glorious union of eternal Fire and Light and Spirit.

In the Kingdom of Heaven these are three and one, because their original, the Holy Trinity, is so and we must call them by the names of Fire and Light and Spirit because all that we have of Fire and Light and Spirit in this world has its whole nature directly from them, and is indeed nothing else but the Fire and Light and Spirit of eternity brought into a separated, compacted, temporal state. So that to speak of a heavenly fire has no more grossness and offence in it than when we speak of a heavenly life, a heavenly light or heavenly spirit, for if there is a heavenly light and spirit there must of all necessity be a heavenly fire; and if these things were not in Heaven in a glorious state of union, they never could have been here in this gross state of a temporal compaction and division. So that as sure as there are fire and light and air in this world, in a

divided, compacted, imperfect state, in which consists the
life of temporary nature and creatures so sure is it that
fire and light and spirit are in the Kingdom of Heaven,
united in one perfection of glory, in which consists the
beatific visibility of God, the divine nature, as communic-
able to heavenly beings.

Now the reason why there are spiritual propertes in all
the material things of this world is only this, it is because
the matter of this world is the materiality of the Kingdom
of Heaven, brought down to a created state of grossness,
death and imprisonment by occasion of the sin of those
Angels who first inhabited the place, or extent of this
material world. Now these heavenly properties which were
brought into this created compaction lie in a continual
desire to return to their first state of glory; and this is the
groaning of the whole creation to be delivered from vanity,
which the Apostle speaks of. And in this continual desire
lieth the kindling and all the possibility of kindling any
fire in the things of this World. Quench this desire and
suppose there is nothing in the matter of this world that
desires to be restored to its first glory, and then all the
breaking forth of fire, light, brightness and glance in the
things of this world is utterly quenched with it, and it
would be the same impossibility to strike fire as to strike
sense and reason out of a flint.

But you will perhaps say, though this be a truth, yet it
is more speculative than edifying, more fitted to entertain
the curiosity than to assist the devotion of Christians. But
stay awhile and you shall see it is a truth full of the most
edifying instruction and directly speaking to the heart.
For if every desire is in itself, in its own essence, the
kindling of fire then we are taught this great practical
lesson, that our own desire is the kindler of our own fire,
the former and raiser of that life which leads us. What our
desire kindles, that becomes the fire of our life, and fits
us either for the majestic glories of the Kingdom of God,

or the dark horrors of Hell. So that our desire is all, it does all, and governs all, and all that we have and are must arise from it, and therefore it is that the Scripture saith, *Keep thy heart with all diligence for out of it are the issues of Life*.

We are apt to think that our imaginations and desires may be played with, that they rise and fall away as nothing, because they do not always bring forth outward and visible effects. But indeed they are the greatest reality we have, and are the true formers and raisers of all that is real and solid in us. All outward power that we exercise in the things about us is but as a shadow in comparison of that inward power that resides in our will, imaginations and desires. These communicate with Eternity and kindle a life which reaches either Heaven or Hell. This strength of the inward man makes all that is the Angel, and all that is the Devil in us, and we are neither good nor bad but according to the working of that which is spiritual and invisible in us. Now our desire is not only thus powerful and productive of real effects, but it is always alive, always working and creating in us, I say creating for it has no less power, it perpetually generates either life or death in us. And here lies the ground of the great efficacy of prayer, which when it is the prayer of the heart, the Prayer of Faith, has a kindling and creating power, and transforms the soul into every thing that its desires reach after. It has the key to the Kingdom of Heaven, and unlocks all its treasures, it opens, extends and moves that in us which has its being and motion in and with the Divine Nature, and so brings us into a real union and communion with God.

III

WE HAVE now, worthy Reader, so far cleared the way that we have nothing to do but to rejoice in the most open illustration and full proof of all the great doctrines of the Gospel, and to see all the objections which Deists, Arians and Socinians have brought against the first Articles of our Faith dashed to pieces. For as soon as we but begin to know that the holy Triune Deity from Eternity to Eternity manifests itself in Nature by the triune birth of fire, light and spirit, and that all Angels and Men must have been created of this Nature, there is not a doctrine in Scripture concerning the Creation, Fall and Redemption of Man, but becomes the most plainly intelligible, and all the Mysteries of our Redemption are proved and confirmed to us by all that is visible and perceptible in all Nature and Creature.

Here we have the plain Foundation of the whole economy of all religion from the beginning to the end of time, why the Incarnation of the Son of God, who is the Light of the World, must have before it the fiery dispensation of the Father delivered from Mount Sinai; and after it, the pouring out or proceeding forth of the Holy Spirit upon all flesh; it is because the triune life of the fallen race must be restored according to the triune manifestation of the Holy Deity in Nature.

Here we know what the love, and what the anger of God is, what Heaven and Hell, an Angel and a Devil, a lost and a redeemed soul are. The love and goodness and blessing of God known, found and enjoyed by any creature is nothing else but the Holy Trinity of God known, found and enjoyed in the blissful, glorious, triune life of fire, light and spirit, where Father, Son and Holy Ghost perpetually communicate their own nameless, numberless, boundless powers, riches and glories to the created image of their own nature.

The Hell in Nature and the hellish life in the creature, the wrath of God in Nature and Creature, is nothing else but the triune holy life broken and destroyed in some order of creatures, it is only the fire of Heaven separated from its heavenly light and spirit. This is that eternal anger and wrath and vengeance that must be atoned, satisfied and removed, that eternal fire that must be quenched, that eternal darkness that must be changed into light, or there is no possibility in nature that the soul of fallen man should ever see the Kingdom of God.

And here all the doctrines of the Socinians are quite torn up by the roots. For in this ground appeareth the absolute necessity of the Incarnation, Life, Sufferings, Death, Resurrection and Ascension of the Son of God. Here lieth the full proof that through all Nature there could no Redeemer of Man be found but only in the Second Person of the adorable Trinity become Man. For as the light and spirit of eternal life is the light and Spirit of the Son and Holy Ghost manifested in Heaven, so the light of Eternal Life could never come again into the fallen soul but from Him alone who is the Light of Heaven. He must be again in the soul as He was in it when it was first breathed forth from the Holy Trinity, He must be manifested in the soul as He was in Heaven, or it can never have the life of Heaven in it. And here we see in the plainest light that there was no anger in God Himself towards the fallen creature, because it was purely and solely the infinite love of God towards him that did, and alone could raise him out of his fallen state. All Scripture as well as Nature obliges us to think thus of God. Thus it is the whole tenor of Scripture that *God so loved the world that He sent His only-begotten Son into it, that the world, through Him, might be saved.* Is not this saying more than if it had been said that there was no anger in God Himself towards fallen man? Is He not expressly declared to be infinitely flowing forth in love towards him? Could God be more infinite in love, or more infinitely distant from all possibility of anger towards man, when He first created him, than when He thus redeemed him?

They therefore who suppose the wrath and anger of God upon fallen man to be a state of mind in God Himself, to be a political kind of just indignation, a point of honourable resentment which the Sovereign Deity, as Governor of the World, ought not to recede from, but must have a sufficient satisfaction done to His offended authority before He can, consistently with His sovereign honour, receive the sinner into His favour, hold the doctrine of the necessity of Christ's atoning Life and Death in a mistaken sense. That many good souls may hold this doctrine in this simplicity of belief, without any more hurt to themselves than others have held the reality of Christ's Flesh and Blood in the Sacrament under the notion of the Transubstantiation of the Bread and Wine I make no manner of doubt. But when books are written to impose and require this belief of others as the only saving Faith in the Life and Death of Christ, it is then an error that ceases to be innocent. For neither reason nor Scripture will allow us to bring wrath unto God Himself as a temper of His mind who is infinite, unalterable, overflowing Love, as unchangeable in love as He is in power and goodness.

The wrath that was awakened at the Fall of Man, that then seized upon him as its captive, was only a plague, or evil or curse that sin had brought forth in Nature and Creature. It was only the beginning of Hell. It was such a wrath as God Himself pitied man's lying under it; it was such a wrath as God Himself furnished man with a power of overcoming and extinguishing, and therefore it was not a wrath that was according to the mind, will and liking, or wisdom of God; and therefore it was not a wrath that was in God Himself, or which was exercised by His sovereign wisdom over His disobedient creatures. It was not such a wrath as when sovereign princes are angry at offenders, and will not cease from their resentment until some political satisfaction or valuable amends be made to their slighted authority.

No, no, it was such a wrath as God Himself hated, as He hates Sin and Hell, a wrath that the God of all Nature and Creature so willed to be removed and extinguished, that seeing nothing less could do it, He sent His only-begotten Son into the world, that all mankind might be saved and delivered from it. For seeing the wrath that was awakened and brought forth by the Fall, and which wanted to be appeased, atoned and quenched was the wrath of eternal Death and eternal Hell that had taken man captive, therefore God spared not the precious, powerful, efficacious Blood of the Holy Jesus, because that alone could extinguish this eternal Wrath of Death and Hell, and re-kindle Heaven and Eternal Life again in the soul. And, thus all the Scriptures speak of the necessity and powerful Atonement of the Life and Death of Christ, all that they say of the infinite Love of God towards fallen man and all that they say of the eternal wrath and vengeance to which man was become a prey have the most solid foundation, and are all of them proved to be consistent, harmonious truths of the greatest certainty, according to the plain letter of Scripture.

God, according to the riches of His Love, raised a man out of the loins of Adam in whose mysterious person the whole humanity and the Word of God was personally united; that same Word which had been inspoken into Adam at his Fall, as a secret Bruiser of the Serpent and real beginning of his salvation, so that in this second Adam, God and Man was one Person. And in this Union of the Divine and human Nature lies the foundation and possibility of our recovery. And seeing also this great and glorious Redeemer had in Himself the whole Humanity, both as it was *before* and after the Fall, *viz*. in His inward man the perfection of the first Adam, and in His outward the weakness and mortality of the fallen nature; and seeing He had all this, as the Undoer of all that Adam had done, as the Overcomer of Death, as the Former and Raiser of our heavenly life, therefore it was that all His conquests over this World, Sin, Death and Hell were not the conquests of a single Person that terminated in Himself, but had their real effect and efficacious merit through *all* human nature, because He was the appointed Father and Regenerator of the whole human nature, and as such had that same relation to it all as Adam had. And therefore as Adam's fall, sin and death did not, could not terminate in himself because he was our appointed Father, from whom we must have such a state and condition of life as he had, so the Righteousness, Death, Resurrection and Ascension of Christ into the Kingdom of Heaven did not terminate in Himself, but became ours because He is our appointed second Adam, from whom we are to derive such a *state* and condition of life as He had; and therefore all that are born again of Him are certainly born into His state of victory and triumph over the World, Sin, Death and Hell.

Now here is opened to us the true reason of the whole process of our Saviour's Incarnation, Passion, Death, Resurrection and Ascension into Heaven. It was because fallen man was to go through all these stages as necessary parts of his return to God, and therefore if man was to go out of his fallen state, there must be a Son of this fallen man who, as a Head and Fountain of the whole race could do all this, could go back through all these gates, and so make it possible for all the individuals of human nature, as being born of Him, to inherit His conquering nature, and follow Him through all these passages to eternal Life. And thus we see, in the strongest and clearest light, both *why* and *how* the holy Jesus is become our great Redeemer.

But I must enlarge a little upon the nature and merits of our Saviour's last sufferings. It is plain from Scripture that that death which our blessed Lord died on the Cross was absolutely necessary for our salvation; that He, as our Saviour, was to taste death for every man; that as the Captain of our Salvation, He was to be made perfect through sufferings; that there was no entrance for fallen man into Paradise till Christ had overcome Death and Hell,

or that first and second Death which stood between us and
it.

Now the absolute necessity of our Saviour's doing and
suffering all this plainly appears as soon as we consider Him
as the second Adam, who, as such, is to undo all the evil
that the first Adam had done in human nature; and therefore must enter into every state that belonged to this
fallen nature, restoring in every state that which was lost,
quickening that which was extinguished, and overcoming in
every state that by which man was overcome. And
therefore as eternal death was as certainly brought forth
in our souls as temporal death in our bodies, as this death
was a state that belonged to fallen man, therefore our Lord
was obliged to taste this dreadful death, to enter into the
realities of it, that He might carry our nature victoriously
through it. And as fallen man was to have entered into
this eternal death at his giving up the ghost in this world, so
the second Adam as reversing all that the first had done,
was to stand in this second death upon the Cross, and die
from it into that Paradise out of which Adam the first died
into this world.

Now when the time drew near that our blessed Lord was
to enter upon His last sufferings, *viz.* the realities of that
second death through which He was to pass, then it was
that all the anguishing terrors of a lost soul began to
open themselves in Him. Then all that eternal death which
Adam had brought into his soul when it lost the light and
spirit of Heaven began to be awakened, and stirring in the
second Adam, who was come to stand in the last state of the
fallen soul, to be encompassed with that eternal death and
sensibility of Hell which must have been the everlasting
state of fallen man. The beginning of our Lord's entrance
into the terrible jaws of this second death may be justly
dated from those affecting words, *My Soul is exceeding
sorrowful even unto Death, tarry ye here with me and watch.*
See here the Lord of Life reduced to such distress as to

beg the prayers, watching and assistance of His poor disciples. A plain proof that it was not the sufferings of this world, but a state of dreadful Dereliction that was coming upon Him.

O holy Redeemer, that I knew how to describe the anguishing terrors of Thy Soul, when Thou wast entering into eternal Death, that no other son of man might fall into it.

The progress of these terrors are plainly shown us in our Lord's Agony in the Garden, when the reality of this eternal death so broke in upon Him, so awakened and stirred itself in Him as to force great drops of Blood to sweat from His Body. This was that bitter cup which made Him withdraw Himself, prostrate Himself and thrice repeat an earnest prayer that if it were possible it might pass from Him, but at the same time heartily prayed to drink it according to the Divine Will. This was that cup He was drinking from the sixth to the ninth hour on the Cross, nailed to the terrors of a two-fold death, when He cried out, *My God, my God, why hast Thou forsaken me?*

We are not to suppose that our Lord's Agony was the terrors of a person that was going to be murdered, or the fears of that death which men could inflict upon Him, for He had told His disciples not to fear them that could only kill the body, and therefore we may be sure that He had no such fears Himself. No, His Agony was His entrance into the last eternal terrors of the lost soul, into the real horrors of that dreadful, eternal death which man unredeemed must have died into when he left this world.

We are therefore not to consider our Lord's Death upon the Cross as only the death of that mortal Body which was nailed to it, but we are to look upon Him with wounded hearts, as fixed and fastened in the state of that two-fold death which was due to the fallen nature out of which He could not come till He could say, *It is finished. Father, into Thy Hands I commend my Spirit.* In that instant

He gave up the ghost of this earthly life, and as a proof of His having overcome all the bars and chains of Death and Hell, He rent the rocks, opened the graves and brought the dead to life, and triumphantly entered into that long shut up Paradise out of which Adam died, and in which He promised the thief he should that day be with Him.

When therefore thou beholdest the Crucifix which finely represents to thy senses the Saviour of the World hanging on the Cross, let not thy thoughts stay on any sufferings, or death that the malice of men can cause, for He hung there in greater distress than any human power can inflict, forsaken of God, feeling, bearing and over-coming the pains and darkness of that eternal Death which the fallen soul of Adam had brought into it.

Lastly, if our blessed Lord was not ascended into Heaven and set on the Right Hand of God, He could not deliver us from our sins, and therefore the Scripture ascribes to Him, as ascended, a perpetual priesthood in Heaven, *If any man sin,* saith St. John, *we have an advocate with the Father, Jesus Christ the Righteous and He is the Propitiation for our Sins.* All these things therefore are so many equally essential parts of our Saviour's character, and He is the one Atonement, the full Satisfaction for Sin, the Saviour and Deliverer from the bondage, power and effects of Sin. And to ascribe our deliverance from Sin, or the remission of our sins more to the Life and Actions than to the Death of Christ, or to His Death more than to His Resurrection and Ascension is directly contrary to the plain letter and tenor of Scripture which speaks of all these things as jointly qualifying our Lord to be the *all-sufficient* Redeemer of Mankind, and when speaking separately of any of them, ascribes the same power, efficacy and redeeming virtue to one as to the other.

Our blessed Lord, who died for us, had not only that outward flesh and blood which He received from the Virgin Mary, and which died upon the Cross, but He had also an holy Humanity of heavenly Flesh and Blood veiled under it, which was appointed by God to quicken, generate and bring forth from itself such an holy offspring of immortal Flesh and Blood as Adam the first should have brought forth before his Fall. Our blessed Lord had a heavenly Humanity which clothed itself with the Flesh·and Blood of this world in the womb of the Virgin, and from that heavenly Humanity, or life-giving Blood it is that our first heavenly, immortal flesh and blood is generated and formed in us again; and therefore His Blood is truly the Atonement, the Ransom, the Redemption, the Life of the World, because it brings forth and generates from itself the paradisaical immortal Flesh and Blood, as certainly, as really, as the blood of fallen Adam brings forth and generates from itself the sinful, vile, corruptible flesh and blood of this Life.

Would you further know what blood this is that has this atoning, life-giving quality in it? It is that Blood which is to be received in the Holy Sacrament.

Would you know why It quickens, raises and restores the inward man that died in Paradise? The answer is from Christ Himself, *He that eateth my Flesh and drinketh my Blood dwelleth in Me and I in him, that is, He is born of my Flesh and Blood*.

Would you know why the Apostle saith, *That He hath purchased us by His Blood*, Acts XX. 28. *That we have Redemption through His Blood*, Ephesians I. 7. Why He prays *The God of Peace, through the Blood of the Everlasting Covenant, to make us perfect in every good work to do His will*; 'Tis because the Holy Jesus saith, *Except we drink His Blood, we have no Life in us*, and therefore the drinking His Blood is the same thing as receiving a life of heavenly Flesh and Blood from Him. And all this is only saying that our Saviour, the second Adam, must do that for us and in us which the first Adam should have done. His Blood must be that to us by way of descent, or birth from Him, which the blood of our first father, if he had not fallen, would have been to us, and as this blood of an immortal life is lost by the Fall, so He from whom we receive It again by a secondary way, is justly and truly saith to purchase, to redeem and ransom by His Blood. Here therefore is plainly discovered to us the true nature, necessity and benefit of the Holy Sacrament of the Lord's Supper, both why and how and for what end we must of all necessity eat the Flesh and drink the Blood of Christ.

No figurative meaning of the words is here to be sought for. We must eat Christ's Flesh and drink His Blood in the same reality as He took upon Him the real flesh and blood of the Blessed Virgin. We can have no real relation to Christ, can be no true members of His Mystical Body but by being real partakers of the same kind of flesh and Blood which was truly His, and was His for this very end, that through Him the same might be brought forth in us.

All this is strictly true of the Holy Sacrament according to the plain letter of the expression, which Sacrament was thus instituted that the great Service of the Church might continually show us that the whole of our Redemption consisted in the receiving the Birth, Spirit, Life and Nature of Jesus Christ into us, in being born of Him, and clothed with a heavenly Flesh and Blood from Him, just as the whole of the Fall consists in our being born of Adam's sinful nature and spirit, and in having a vile, corrupt and impure flesh and blood from him. And thus we have the plain and full truth of the most mysterious part of this Holy Sacrament, delivered from the tedious strife of words and that thickness of darkness which learned contenders on all sides have brought into it. The letter and spirit of Scripture are here both preserved, and the Mystery appears so amiable, so intelligible and so beneficial as must needs raise a true and earnest devotion in everyone that is capable of hungering and thirsting after Eternal Life.

And this true and sound knowledge of the Holy Sacrament could never have been lost if this Scripture truth had not been overlooked, namely, that Christ is our Second Adam, that He is to do that for us which Adam should have done, that we are to have that life from Him, as a quickening spirit, which we should have had from Adam as a living soul, and that our Redemption is only doing a second time or in a second way, that which should have been done by the first order of our creation. This plain doctrine attended to would sufficiently show us that the Flesh and Blood of Eternal Life, which we are to receive from Christ, must be that flesh and blood of Eternal Life which we lost in Adam. Now if we had this immortal Flesh and Blood by our descent from Adam, we must in the strictness of the expression have been said to partake of the flesh and blood of Adam, so seeing we *now* receive It from Christ, we must in the same strictness of expression, be said to be real partakers of the Flesh and Blood of Christ, because He hath the same heavenly flesh and blood which Adam had, and for the same end that Adam had it, namely that it may come by and through Him into us.

And thus is this great Sacrament which is a continual part of our Christian worship a continual communication to us of all the benefits of our Second Adam; for in and by the Body and Blood of Christ, to which the Divine Nature is united, we receive all that Life, Immortality and Redemption which Christ as living, suffering, dying, rising from the dead and ascending into Heaven, brought to human nature so that this great Mystery is that in which all the blessings of our Redemption and new life in Christ are centred. And they that hold a Sacrament short of this Reality of the true Body and Blood of Jesus Christ cannot be said to hold that Sacrament of Eternal Life which was instituted by our Blessed Lord and Saviour.

THE SPIRIT OF PRAYER

OR

THE SOUL RISING OUT OF THE VANITY OF TIME INTO THE RICHES OF ETERNITY

By WILLIAM LAW, M.A.

(Abridged)

CONTENTS

Part the First

Part the First

I

THE GREATEST part of mankind, nay of Christians, may be said to be asleep, and that particular way of life which takes up each man's mind, thoughts and actions may be very well called his particular dream. This degree of vanity is equally visible in every form and order of life. The learned and the ignorant, the rich and the poor are all in the same state of slumber, only passing away a short life in a different kind of dream.

But why so?

It is because man has an eternity within him, is born into this world, not for the sake of living here, not for any thing this world can give him, but only to have time and place to become either an eternal partaker of a divine life with God, or to have an hellish eternity among fallen Angels. And, therefore, every man who has not his eye, his heart and his hands continually governed by this two-fold eternity may be justly said to be fast asleep, to have no awakened sensibility of himself.

And a life devoted to the interests and enjoyments of this world, spent and wasted in the slavery of earthly desires, may be truly called a dream, as having all the shortness, vanity and delusion of a dream, only with this great difference, that when a dream is over, nothing is lost but fictions and fancies, but when the dream of life is ended only by death, all that eternity is lost for which we were brought into being.

Do but suppose a man to know himself, that he comes into this world on no other errand but to rise out of the vanity of time into the riches of eternity; do but suppose him to govern his inward thoughts and outward actions by this view of himself, and then to him every day has lost all its evil, prosperity and adversity have no difference because he receives and uses them both in the same spirit. Life and death are equally welcome because equally parts of his way to eternity. For poor and miserable as this life is, we have all of us free access to all that is great and good and happy, and carry within ourselves a key to all the treasures that Heaven has to bestow upon us. For Heaven is as near to our souls as this world is to our bodies, and we are created, we are redeemed to have our conversation in it.

God, the only Good of all intelligent natures, is not an absent or distant God, but is more present in and to our souls than our own bodies, and we are strangers to Heaven and without God in the world for this only reason, because we are void of that Spirit of Prayer which alone can, and never fails to unite us with the One Only Good, and to open Heaven and the Kingdom of God within us.

A root set in the finest soil, in the best climate, and blessed with all that sun and air and rain can do for it, is not in so sure a way of its growth to perfection as every man may be whose spirit aspires after all that which God is ready and infinitely desirous to give him. For the sun meets not the springing bud that stretches towards him with half that certainty that God, the source of all Good, communicates Himself to the soul that longs to partake of Him.

We are all of us, by birth, the offspring of God, more nearly related to Him than we are to one another, for in Him *we live and move and have our being.*

The first man that was brought forth from God had the Breath and Spirit of Father, Son and Holy Ghost breathed into him, and so he became a living soul. Thus was our first father born of God, descended from Him, and stood in Paradise in the image and likeness of God. He was the image and likeness of God, not with any regard to his outward shape or form, for no shape has any likeness to God, but he was in the image and likeness of God because the Holy Trinity had breathed their own nature and spirit into him. And as the Deity, Father, Son and Holy Spirit, are always in Heaven and make Heaven to be everywhere, so this Spirit breathed by them into man, brought Heaven into man along with it, and so man was in Heaven as well as on earth, that is, in Paradise, which signifies an heavenly state or birth of life.

Adam had all that divine nature both as to an heavenly spirit and heavenly body which the Angels have. But as he was brought forth to be a lord and ruler of a new world, created out of the chaos or ruins of the kingdom of fallen Angels, so it was necessary that he should also have the nature of this new created world in himself, both as to its spirit and materiality. Hence it was that he had a body taken from this new created earth, not such dead earth as we now make bricks of, but the blessed earth of Paradise that had the power of Heaven in it, out of which the Tree of Life itself could grow.

Into the nostrils of this outward body was the breath or spirit of this world breathed, and in this spirit and body of this world did the inward celestial spirit and body of Adam dwell. It was the medium or means through which he was to have commerce with this world, become visible to its creatures, and rule over it and them. Thus stood our first father, an Angel, both as to body and spirit (as he will be again after the Resurrection) yet dwelling in a body and spirit taken from this new created world which, however, was as inferior to him, as subject to him, as the earth and all its creatures were. It was no more alive in him, no more brought forth its nature within him than Satan and the Serpent were alive in him at his first creation. And herein lay the ground of Adam's ignorance of good and evil.

It was because his outward body and the outward world (in which alone was good and evil) could not discover their own nature, or open their own life within him, but were kept inactive by the power and life of the celestial man within it. And this was man's first and great trial, a trial not imposed upon him by the mere Will of God, or by way of experiment, but a trial necessarily implied in the nature of his state. He was created an Angel, both as to body and spirit, and this Angel stood in an outward body, of the nature of the outward world, and therefore by the nature of his state he had his trial, or power of choosing whether he would live as an Angel, using only his outward body as a means of opening the wonders of the outward world to the glory of his Creator, or whether he would turn his desire to the opening of the bestial life of the outward worldling himself, for the sake of knowing the good and evil that was in it.

The fact is certain that he lusted after the knowledge of this good and evil, and made use of the means to obtain it. No sooner had he got this knowledge, by the opening the bestial life and sensibility within him, but in that day, nay in that instant, he died, that is, his heavenly spirit with its heavenly body were both extinguished in him, but his soul, and immortal fire that could not die, became a poor slave in prison of bestial flesh and blood.

See here the nature and necessity of our Redemption. It is to redeem the first angelic nature that departed from Adam. It is to make that heavenly spirit and body which Adam lost, to be alive again in all the human nature. And this is called *Regeneration*.

The necessity of our regaining our first heavenly body is the necessity of our eating the Body and Blood of Christ. The necessity of having again our first heavenly spirit is declared by the necessity of our being baptized by the Holy Ghost.

Our Fall is nothing else but the falling of our soul from

this celestial body and spirit into a bestial body and spirit of this world. Our rising out of our fallen state, or Redemption, is nothing else but the regaining our first angelic spirit and body, which in Scripture is called our inward, or new man, created again in Christ Jesus.

See here, lastly, the true ground of all the mortifications of flesh and blood required in the Gospel. It is because this bestial life of this outward world should not have been opened in man. It is his separation from God, and death to the Kingdom of Heaven, and therefore all its workings, appetites and desires are to be restrained and kept under, that the first heavenly life to which Adam died, may have room to rise up in us.

Let us now consider some plain and important Truths that follow from what has been said above. First, it is plain that the sin and fall of Adam did not consist in this, *viz.* that he had only committed a single act of disobedience, and so might have been just as he was before if God had pleased to overlook this single act of disobedience and not to have brought a curse upon him and his posterity for it. Nothing of this is the truth of the matter, either on the part of God, or on the part of man. Secondly, it is plain also that the command of God not to lust after and eat of the Forbidden Tree was not an arbitrary command of God, given at pleasure, or as a mere trial of man's obedience, but was a most kind and living information given by the God of Love to his new-born offspring concerning the state he was in with regard to the outward world. Warning him to withdraw all desire of entering into a sensibility of its good and evil, because such sensibility could not be had without his immediate dying to that divine and heavenly life which he then enjoyed. '*Eat not,*' says the God of Love, '*of the Tree of Knowledge of good and evil, for in the day thou eatest thereof thou wilt surely die.*' Thirdly, that the misery, distress and woeful condition which Adam by his transgression brought upon himself and all his posterity was not the effect of any severe vindictive wrath in God, calling for justice to his offended sovereignty and inflicting pains and punishments suitable to the greatness of His indignation and anger at the disobedient creature.

If Adam contrary to the Will of God, and for the sake of some new-fancied knowledge had broken both his own legs and put out both his eyes, could it with any show of truth and reason have been said that God, in the severity of His wrath at so heinous an offence, had punished Adam with lameness and blindness?

And if it be further supposed that God, seeing Adam lying in this lame and blind condition, came and spoke kindly to him, informing him of a secret of love which He had in Heaven, which He promised to send him immediately by His Highest Messenger of Love, assuring him that the use of this heavenly secret or divine power his legs and eyes should in some course of time be infallibly restored to him, even in a better state than they were in at the first, must it not be still more unreasonable and absurd to charge anything of this lameness and blindness upon a wrath in God kindled against Adam? Nay, is it not clear in the highest degree that in all this matter Adam had nothing from God but the overflowings of mere love and goodness, and that he had no lameness and blindness but from his own voluntary acts upon himself?

This is a simple but clear representation of the case, how matters stood betwixt God and our first father when by his own act and deed he extinguished that divine life in which God had created him. Adam had no more hurt, no more evil done to him at his Fall than the very nature of his own action brought along with it upon himself. He lusted to have the sensibility of that good and evil which the beasts of this world have. He was told that it could not be had without the loss of his Heavenly life, because such loss was as necessarily implied in the nature of the thing itself, as blindness is implied in the extinction of eyes. However, he ventured to make the trial, and chose to eat of that which could and did open this sensibility of earthly good and evil in him. No sooner was this sensibility opened in him but he found it to be a subjection and slavery to all outward nature, to heat and cold, to pains and sickness, horror of mind, disturbed passions, misery, and fears of death. Which is in other words only saying that he found it to be an extinction of that divine, angelical nature which till then had kept him insensible and incapable of any hurtful impressions from any or all the powers of this world. Therefore, to charge his miserable state as a punishment inflicted upon him by the severe wrath of an incensed God is the same absurdity as in the former supposed lameness and blindness. Because the whole nature of all that miserable change, both as to body and soul, which then came upon him, was neither more nor less than what was necessarily implied in that which he chose to do to himself. And therefore it had nothing of the nature of a punishment inflicted from without, but was only that which his own action had done in and to himself, just as the man who puts out his own eyes has only the darkness and blindness which his own action has brought forth in himself.

From this short, and yet plain and true account of this matter, we are at once delivered from a load of difficulties that have been raised about the Fall of Man, and Original Sin. It has been a great question How the goodness of God could punish so small and single an act of disobedience in Adam with so great a punishment? Here the sovereignty of God has been appealed to and has set the matter right, and from this sovereignty thus asserted came forth the systems of absolute Election and absolute Reprobation. But for our comfort it appears that the question here put concerns neither God nor Man, that it relates not at all to the matter, and has no existence but in the brains of those that formed it. For the action in which Adam's sin consisted was such an act as in itself implied all that miserable change that came upon him, and so was not a small, or single act of disobedience, nor had the least punishment of any kind inflicted by God upon it. All that God did on this transgression was mere love, compassion and relief administered to it. All the sovereignty that God here showed was a sovereignty of Love to the fallen creature. So that all the volumes on this question may be laid aside as quite beside the point.

Another, and the greatest question of all, and which Divines of all sorts have been ever solving and yet never have solved, is this. *How can it consist with the Goodness of God to impute the Sin of Adam to all his posterity?* But here, to our comfort again, it may be said that this question is equally a vain fiction with the other, and has nothing to do with the procedure of God towards mankind. For there is no imputation of the sin of Adam to his posterity and so no foundation for a dispute upon it. How absurd would it be to say that God imputes the nature, or the body and soul of Adam to his posterity? For have they not the nature of Adam by a natural birth from him, and not by imputation from God? Now this is all the sin that Adam's posterity have from him, they have only their flesh and blood, their body and soul from him, by a birth and not imputed to them from God.

Instead, therefore, of the former question which is quite beside the matter, it should have been asked thus, *How was it consistent with the Goodness of God that Adam could not generate children of a nature and kind quite superior to himself?* This is the only question that can be asked in relation to God, and yet it is a question whose absurdity confutes itself. For the only reason why sin is found in the sons of Adam is this, it is because Adam of earthly flesh and blood cannot bring forth a holy Angel out of himself, but must beget children of the same nature and condition with himself. And therefore, here again it may be truly said that all the laborious volumes on God's imputing

Adam's sin to his posterity ought to be considered as waste paper.

But further, as it is thus evident from the nature of Adam's trangresssion that all his misery came from the nature of his own action, and that nothing was inflicted upon him from a wrath or anger in God at him, so is it still much more so from a consideration of the Divine Nature. For it is a glorious and joyful truth (however suppressed in various systems of divinity) that from eternity to eternity no spark of wrath ever was or ever will be in the holy Triune God. If a wrath of God was anywhere it must be everywhere, if it burned once it must burn to all eternity. For everything that is in God Himself is boundless, incapable of any increase or diminution without beginning and without end. It is as good sense, as consistent with the Divine Nature to say that God, moved by a wrath in and from Himself, began the Creation, as that a wrath in God ever punished any part of it.

Nature and Creature is the only source from whence, and the seat in which, wrath, pain and vexation can dwell. Nor can they ever break forth either in nature or creature, but so far as either this or that has lost its state in God. This is as certain as that storms and tempests, thunder and lightnings, have no existence in Heaven. God, considered in Himself, is as infinitely separate from all possibility of doing hurt, or willing pain to any creature, as He is from a possibility of suffering pain or hurt from the hand of man. And this, for this plain reason, because He is in Himself, in His Holy Trinity, nothing else but the boundless abyss of all that is good and sweet and amiable, and therefore stands in the utmost contrariety to every thing that is not a blessing, in an eternal impossibility of willing and intending a moment's pain or hurt to any creature. For from this unbounded Source of goodness and perfection, nothing but infinite streams of blessing are perpetually flowing forth upon all Nature and Creature in a more incessant plenty than rays of light stream from the sun. And as the sun has but one nature, and can give forth nothing but the blessings of light, so the Holy Triune God has but one nature and intent towards all the Creation, which is, to pour forth the riches and sweetness of His divine perfections upon every thing that is capable of them, and according to its capacity to receive them.

The goodness of God breaking forth into a desire to communicate good was the cause and the beginning of the Creation. Hence it follows that to all eternity, God can have no thought or intent towards the creature but to communicate good, because He made the creature for this sole end, to receive good. The first motive towards the creature is unchangeable. It takes its rise from God's desire to communicate good, and it is an eternal impossibility that anything can ever come from God as His will and purpose towards the creature, but that same love and goodness which first created it. He must always *will* that to it which He willed at the creation of it. This is the amiable nature of God, He is the good, the unchangeable, overflowing Fountain of Good that sends forth nothing but good to all eternity. He is the Love itself, the unmixed unmeasurable Love, doing nothing but from love, giving nothing but gifts of love to every thing that He has made; requiring nothing of all His creatures but the spirit and fruits of that love which brought them into being. Oh, how sweet is this contemplation of the height and depth of the riches of Divine Love! With what attraction must it draw every thoughtful man to return love for love to this overflowing Fountain of boundless goodness. What charms has that religion which discovers to us our existence in relation to and dependence upon this ocean of Divine Love! View every part of our Redemption, from Adam's first sin to the Resurrection of the Dead, and you will find nothing but successive Mysteries of that first Love which created Angels and men. All the Mysteries of the Gospel are only so many marks or proofs of God's desiring to make His love triumph in the removal of sin and disorder from all nature and creature.

See here the deep ground and absolute necessity of that new birth of Word, Son and Spirit which the Scripture speaks so much of. It is because our soul, as fallen, is quite dead to and separate from the Kingdom of Heaven by having lost the light and spirit of God in itself, and therefore it is and must be incapable of entering into Heaven till by this new birth, the soul again gets its first Heavenly nature. If thou hast nothing of this birth when thy body dies, then thou hast only that root of life in thee which the Devils have. Thou art as far from Heaven and incapable of it as they are. Thy nature is their nature, and therefore their habitation must be thine. For nothing can possibly hinder thy union with fallen angels when thou diest, but a birth of that in thy soul which the fallen angels have lost.

How pitiable therefore, or rather how hurtful is that learning which uses all its art of words to avoid and lose the true sense of our Saviour's doctrine concerning the new birth, which is necessary to fallen man by holding that the passages asserting the new birth are only a figurative strong form of words concerning something that is not really a birth or growth of a new nature, but may, according to the best rules of criticism signify either our entrance into the Society of Christians by the Rite of Baptism, or such a new relation, as a scholar may have with his master, who by conformity to terms of union, or by copying his ways and manners may, by a figure of speech, be said to be born again of him.

Now let it here be observed that no passage of Scripture is to be called, or esteemed as a figurative expression but where the literal meaning cannot be allowed as implying something that is either bad in itself, or impossible, or inconsistent with some plain and undeniable doctrines of

Scripture. Now that this is not the case here is very evident. For who will presume to say that for the soul of fallen man to be born again of the Son, or Light, and Holy Spirit of God, is in the literal sense of the word, a thing bad in itself, or impossible, or inconsistent with any plain and undeniable doctrines of Scripture? The critics therefore who in this matter leave the literal meaning of the words, and have recourse to a figurative sense, are without excuse, and have nothing they can urge as a reason for so doing, but their own skill in words. But it may be further added as a just charge against these critics that their fixing these passages to a figurative meaning is not only without any ground or reason for so doing, but it is also a bad meaning impossible to be true and utterly inconsistent with the most plain and fundamental doctrines of Scripture. Now that this is the case here may in part be seen by the following instance.

Let it be supposed that a human body had lost the light, and air of this world, and was in a state of death, because both these were quite extinguished in it. Must it not be said that this human body cannot see or enter again into the life of this world unless the light and air of this world get again a new birth in it. Is there here any occasion or any room to form a doubt how these words are to be understood, or any possibility to mistake the meaning of them? What a philosopher would he be who for fear of being called an enthusiast should here deny the literal meaning of a new birth of light and air, and think himself sufficiently justified in flying from it because in his great reading he had seen the words, birth, light and air sometimes, and upon some occasions used only in a figurative sense? Now this is exactly, and to a tittle, the case of the soul, as fallen, and lying in the same state of death to the Kingdom of God till a new birth of the light and spirit of God be again brought forth in it. And therefore the necessity of understanding these words in their literal meaning, the absurdity of flying to a figurative sense of the new birth, and the impossibility of that being the true one is equally plain and certain in both these cases.

Now that the soul, as fallen, is in this real state of death is a doctrine not only plain from the whole tenor of Scripture, but affirmed in all systems of divinity. For all hold and teach that man unredeemed, must at the death of his body have fallen into a state of misery like that of the fallen angels. But how can this be true unless it be true that the life of Heaven was extinguished in the soul, and that man had really lost that light and spirit of God which alone can make any being capable of living in Heaven. All therefore that I have here and elsewhere said concerning the death of the soul by its fall, and its wanting a real new birth of the Son and Holy Spirit of God in it, in order to its salvation, cannot be denied, but by giving up this great, fundamental doctrine, namely, *'that man in his fallen state and unredeemed must have been eternally lost.'* For it cannot be true that the fall of man, unredeemed, would have kept him for ever out of Heaven, but because his fall had absolutely put an end to the life of Heaven in his soul.

On the other hand, it cannot be true that Jesus Christ is his Redeemer, and does deliver him from his fallen state unless it be true that Jesus Christ helps him to a new birth of that light and spirit of God which was extinguished by his fall. For nothing could possibly be the redemption or recovery of man but Regeneration alone. His misery was his having lost the life and light of Heaven from his soul and therefore nothing in all the universe of Nature but a new birth of that which he had lost could be his deliverance from his fallen state. And therefore if angels after angels had come down from Heaven to assure him that God had no anger at him, he would still have been in the same helpless state; nay, had they told him that God had pity and compassion towards him, he had yet been unhelped because in the nature of the thing nothing could make so much as a beginning of his deliverance, but that which made a beginning of a new birth in him, and nothing could fully effect his recovery, but which perfectly finished the new birth of all that heavenly life which he had lost.

Let no one here think to charge me with disregard to the Holy Jesus, who was born of the Virgin Mary, or with setting up an inward Saviour in opposition to that outward Christ whose history is recorded in the Gospel. No, it is with the utmost fulness of faith and assurance that I ascribe all our Redemption to that blessed and mysterious Person that was then born of the Virgin Mary and will assert no inward Redemption but what wholly proceeds from, and is effected by that Life-giving Redeemer who died on the Cross for our Redemption.

Was I to say that a plant or vegetable must have the sun within it, must have the life, light and virtues of the sun incorporated in it, that it has no benefit from the sun till the sun is thus inwardly forming, generating, quickening and raising up a life of the sun's virtues in it, would this be setting up an inward sun in opposition to the outward one? Could anything be more ridiculous than such a charge? For is not all that is here said of an inward sun in the vegetable so much said of a power and virtue derived from the sun in the firmament? So in like manner all that is said of an inward Christ, inwardly formed and generated in the root of the soul, is only so much said of an inward life, brought forth by the power and efficacy of the Blessed Christ that was born of the Virgin Mary.

II

THOU HAST seen, dear Reader, the nature and necessity of Regeneration, be persuaded therefore fully to believe and firmly to settle in thy mind this most certain truth, that all our salvation consists in the manifestation of the nature, life and spirit of Jesus Christ, in our inward new man. This alone is Christian Redemption, this alone delivers from the guilt and power of sin, this alone redeems, renews and regains the first life of God in the soul of man. Every thing besides this is self, is fiction, is propriety, is own will, and however coloured is only thy old man, with all his deeds. Enter therefore with all thy heart into this truth, let thy eye be always upon it, do everything in view of it, try everything by the truth of it, love nothing but for the sake of it.

Wherever thou goest, whatever thou dost, at home or abroad or in the field, or at Church, do all in a desire of union with Christ, in imitation of His tempers and inclinations, and look upon all as nothing, but that which exercises and increases the spirit and life of Christ in thy soul. From morning to night keep Jesus in thy heart, long for nothing, desire nothing, hope for nothing but to have all that is within thee changed into the spirit and temper of the Holy Jesus. Let this be thy Christianity, thy Church and thy Religion. For this new birth in Christ thus firmly believed and continually desired, will do every thing that thou wantest to have done in thee, it will dry up all the springs of vice, stop all the workings of evil in thy nature, it will bring all that is good into thee, it will open all the Gospel within thee, and thou wilt know what it is to be taught of God. This longing desire of thy heart to be one with Christ will soon put a stop to all the vanity of thy life, and nothing will be admitted to enter into thy heart, or proceed from it, but what comes from God and returns to God. Thou wilt soon be, as it were, tied and bound in the chains of all holy affections and desires, thy mouth will have a watch set upon it, thy ears would willingly hear nothing that does not tend to God, nor thy eyes be open but to see and find occasions of doing good. In a word, when this faith has got both thy head and thy heart, it will then be with thee as it was with the merchant who found the pearl of great price, it will make thee gladly to sell all that thou hast and buy it.

But thou wilt perhaps say, How shall this great work, the birth of Christ, be effected in me? It might rather be said that since Christ has infinite power, and also an infinite desire to save mankind, how can anyone miss of this salvation, but through his own unwillingness to be saved by Him? Consider, how was it that the lame and blind, the lunatic and leper, the publican and sinner found Christ to be their Saviour, and to do all that for them which they wanted to be done to them? It was because they had a real desire of having that which they asked for, and therefore in true faith and prayer applied to Christ that His spirit and power might enter into them, and heal that which they wanted, and desired to be healed in them. Every one of these said in faith and desire 'Lord, if Thou wilt, Thou canst make me whole.' And the answer was always this, 'According to thy faith, so be it done unto thee.' This is Christ's answer *now* and thus it is done to every one of us at this day, as our faith is, so is it done unto us. And here lies the whole reason of our falling short of the salvation of Christ it is because we have no will to it.

But you will say, Do not all Christians desire to have Christ to be their Saviour? Yes. But here is the deceit. All would have Christ to be their Saviour in the next world and to help them into Heaven when they die, by His power and merits with God. But this is not *willing* Christ to be thy Saviour, for His salvation, if it is is had, must be had in this world. If He saves thee, it must be done in this life, by changing and altering all that is within thee, by helping thee to a new heart, as He helped the blind to see, the lame to walk and the dumb to speak. For to have salvation from Christ is nothing else but to be made like unto Him. It is to have His humility and meekness, His mortification and self-denial, His renunciation of the spirit, wisdom, and honours of this world, His love of God, His desire of doing God's will and seeking only His honour. To have these tempers formed and begotten to thy heart is to have salvation from Christ. But if thou willest not to have these tempers brought forth in thee, if thy faith and desire does not seek and cry to Christ for them in the same reality as the lame asked to walk, and the blind to see, then thou must be said to be unwilling to have Christ to be thy Saviour.

But to return. It is manifest that no one can fail of the benefit of Christ's salvation, but through an unwillingness to have it, and from the same spirit and tempers which made the Jews unwilling to receive it. But if thou wouldest still further know how this great work, this birth of Christ, is to be effected in thee, then let this joyful truth be told thee, that this great work is already begun in every one of us. For this Holy Jesus that is to be formed in thee, that is to be the Saviour and new Life of thy Soul, that is to raise thee out of the darkness of death unto the light of life, and give thee power to become a son of God, is already within thee, living, stirring, calling, knocking at the door of thy heart and wanting nothing but thy own faith and good will, to have as real a birth and form in thee, as He had in the Virgin Mary.

For the Eternal Word, or Son of God, did not then first begin to be the Saviour of the World when He was born in Bethlehem of Judaea, but that Word which became Man in the Virgin Mary did, from the beginning of the world, enter as a Word of Life, a Seed of Salvation into the first father of mankind, was inspoken into him as an ingrafted Word under the name and character of a Bruiser of the Serpent's head. Hence it is that Christ said to His disciples *'The Kingdom of God is within you,'* that is, the Divine Nature is within you given unto your first father, into the light of his life, and from him, rising up in the life of every son of Adam. Hence also the Holy Jesus is said to be the *'Light which lighteth every man that cometh into the world.'* Not as He was born at Bethlehem, not as He had an human form upon earth, in these respects He could not be said to have been the light of every man that cometh into the world, but as He was that Eternal Word, by which all things were created, which was the Life and Light of all things, and which had as a second Creator entered again into fallen man, as a Bruiser of the Serpent. In this respect it was truly said of our Lord when on earth that *'He was that Light that lighteth every man that cometh into the World.'* For He was really and truly all this, as He was the Immanuel, the God with us given unto Adam, and in him to all his offspring.

See here the beginning and glorious extent of the Catholic Church of Christ, it takes in all the world. It is God's unlimited universal mercy to all mankind, and every human creature as sure as he was born of Adam, has a birth of the Bruiser of the Serpent within him, and so is infallibly in covenant with God through Jesus Christ. Hence also it is that the Holy Jesus is appointed to be Judge of all the world, it is because all mankind, all nations and languages have in Him and through Him been put into covenant with God, and made capable of resisting the evil of their fallen nature.

Poor sinner, consider the treasure thou hast within thee, the Saviour of the World, the eternal Word of God lies hid in thee, as a spark of the Divine Nature which is to overcome sin and death and hell within thee, and generate the life of Heaven again in thy soul. Turn to thy heart, and thy heart will find its Saviour, its God within itself. Thou seest, hearest and feelest nothing of God because thou seekest for Him abroad with thy outward eyes, thou seekest for Him in books, in controversies, in the Church and outward exercises, but there thou wilt not find Him till thou hast first found Him in thy heart. Seek for Him in thy heart, and thou wilt never seek in vain, for there He dwells, there is the seat of His light and Holy Spirit. For this turning to the light and Spirit of God within thee is thy only true turning unto God, there is not other way of finding Him, but in that place where He dwelleth in thee. For though God be everywhere present, yet He is only present to thee in the deepest and most central part of thy soul. Thy natural senses cannot possess God, or unite thee to Him, nay thy inward faculties of understanding, will and memory can only reach after God, but cannot be the place of His habitation in thee. But there is a root or depth in thee from whence all these faculties come forth, as lines from a centre, or as branches from the body of the tree. This depth is called the Centre, the Fund, or Bottom of the soul. This depth is the unity, the eternity, I had almost said, the infinity of thy soul, for it is so infinite that nothing can satisfy it, or give it any rest, but the infinity of God.

In this depth of the soul, the Holy Trinity brought forth its own living image in the first created man, bearing in himself a representation of Father, Son and Holy Ghost, and this was his dwelling in God and God in him. This was the Kingdom of God within him and made Paradise without him. But the day that Adam did eat of the forbidden earthly tree, in that day he absolutely died to this Kingdom of God within him. This depth or centre of his soul having lost its God, was shut up in death and darkness, and became a prisoner in an earthly animal that only excelled its brethren, the beasts, in an upright form and serpentine subtilty. Thus ended the Fall of Man. But from that moment the God of Mercy inspoke into Adam the bruiser of the serpent, from that moment all the riches and treasures of the Divine Nature came again into man, as a Seed of Salvation sown into the centre of the soul, and only lies hidden there in every man till he desires to rise from his fallen state and be born again from above.

Awake then, thou that sleepest, and Christ who from all eternity has been espoused to thy soul shall give thee light.

Begin to search and dig in thine own field for this Pearl of Eternity that lies hidden in it. It cannot cost thee too much nor canst thou buy it too dear, for it is *all* and when thou hast found it, thou wilt know that all which thou hast sold or given away for it is as mere a nothing as a bubble upon the water.

When this Seed of the Spirit, common to all men, is not resisted, grieved and quenched, but its inspirations and motives suffered to grow and increase in us, to unite with God and get power over all the lusts of the flesh, then we are born again, the nature, spirit and tempers of Jesus Christ are opened in our souls, the Kingdom of God is come and is found within us. On the other hand, when the flesh or the natural man has resisted and quenched this Spirit or Seed of Life within us, then the works of the flesh, adultery, fornication, murders, lying, hatred, envy, wrath, pride, foolishness, worldly wisdom, carnal prudence, false religion, hypocritical holiness, and serpentine subtilty have set up their kingdom within us.

See here in short the state of man as redeemed. He has a spark of the light and Spirit of God, as a supernatural gift of God given into the birth of his soul, to bring forth by degrees a New Birth of that life which was lost in Paradise. This Holy Spark of the Divine Nature within him has a natural, strong and almost infinite tendency, or reaching after that eternal light and spirit of God from whence it came forth. It came forth from God, it came out of God, it partaketh of the Divine Nature and therefore it is always in a state of tendency and return to God. And all this is called the breathing, the moving, the quickening of the Holy Spirit within us, which are so many operations of this Spark of Life tending towards God. On the other hand, the Deity as considered in itself, and without the soul of man, has an infinite, unchangeable tendency of love, and desire towards the soul of man, to unite and communicate its own riches and glories to it, just as the spirit of the air without man, unites and communicates its riches and virtues to the spirit of the air that is within man. This love, or desire of God towards the soul of man is so great that He gave His only-begotten Son, the Brightness of His Glory, to take the human nature upon Him, in its fallen state, that by this mysterious union of God and Man, all the enemies of the soul of man might be overcome, and every human creature might have a power of being born again according to that image of God in which he was first created.

The Gospel is the history of this Love of God to Man.

Inwardly, he has a seed of the Divine Life given into the birth of his soul, a seed that has all the riches of eternity in it, and is always wanting to come to the birth in him, and be alive in God. Outwardly he has Jesus Christ, who as a Sun of Righteousness, is always casting forth His enlivening beams on this inward seed, to kindle and call it forth to the birth, doing that to this seed of Heaven in man which the sun in the firmament is always doing to the vegetable seeds in the earth.

Consider this matter in the following similitude. A grain of wheat has the air and light of this world inclosed, or incorporated in it. This is the mystery of its life, this is its power of growing, by this it has a strong continual tendency of uniting again with that ocean of light and air from whence it came forth and so it helps to kindle its own vegetable life. On the other hand, that great ocean of light and air, having its own offspring hidden in the heart of the grain, has a perpetual strong tendency to unite and communicate with it again. From this desire of union on both sides, the vegetable life arises and all the virtues and powers contained in it.

But here let it be well observed, that this desire on both sides cannot have its effect till the husk and gross part of the grain falls into a state of corruption and death. Till this begins the mystery of life hidden in it cannot come forth.

The application here may be left to the reader. I shall only observe that we may here see the true ground and absolute necessity of that dying to ourselves, and to the world, to which our Blessed Lord so constantly calls all His followers. A universal self-denial, a perpetual mortification of the lust of the flesh, the lust of the eyes, and the pride of life, is not a thing imposed upon us by the mere Will of God, is not required as a punishment, is not an invention of dull and monkish spirits, but has its ground and reason in the nature of the thing, and is as absolutely necessary to make way for the new birth, as the death of the husk and gross part of the grain is necessary to make way for its vegetable life.

But secondly, this Pearl of Eternity is the wisdom and love of God within thee. In this Pearl of thy Serpent Bruiser, all the holy nature, spirit, tempers, and inclinations of Christ lie as in a seed in the centre of thy soul, and divine Wisdom and heavenly Love will grow up in thee, if thou givest but true attention to God present in thy soul. On the other hand, there is hidden also in the depth of thy nature the root or possibility of all the hellish nature, spirit and tempers of the fallen angels. For Heaven and Hell have each of them their foundation within us, they come not into us from without, but spring up in us according as our will and heart is turned either to the Light of God, or the Kingdom of Darkness. But when this life, which is in the midst of these two eternities, is at an end, either an Angel, or a Devil will be found to have a birth in us.

And thirdly, this Pearl of Eternity is the Church, or Temple of God within thee, the consecrated place of Divine Worship where alone thou canst worship God in spirit and in truth. In spirit, because thy spirit is that alone in thee which can unite and cleave unto God and receive the workings of His Divine Spirit upon thee. In truth, because this adoration in spirit is that truth and reality of which all outward forms and rites, though instituted by God are only the figure for a time, but this worship is eternal. Accustom thyself to the holy service of this inward Temple. In the midst of it is the Fountain of Living Water, of which thou mayest drink, and live for ever. There the mysteries of thy Redemption are celebrated, or rather opened in life and power. There the Supper of the Lamb is kept, the Bread that came down from Heaven, that giveth life to the World, is thy true nourishment. All is done and known in real experience, in a living sensibility of the work of God in the soul. There the birth, the life, the sufferings, the death, the Resurrection and Ascension of Christ are not merely remembered but inwardly found and enjoyed as the real states of thy soul, which has followed Christ in the Regeneration. When once thou art well grounded in this inward worship, thou wilt have learnt to live unto God above time and place. For every day will be Sunday to thee, and wherever thou goest, thou wilt have a Priest, a Church, and an Altar along with thee. For when God has all that He should have of thy heart, when renouncing the will, judgment, tempers and inclinations of the old man, thou art wholly given up to the obedience of the light and spirit of God within thee, to will only His Holy Will, to love only in His love, to be wise only in His wisdom, then it is that every thing thou doest is as a song of praise, and the common business of thy life is a conforming to God's will on earth, as Angels do in Heaven.

Fourthly and lastly, this Pearl of Eternity is the peace and joy of God within thee, but can only be found by the manifestation of the life and power of Jesus Christ in thy soul. But Christ cannot be thy power and thy life till in obedience to His call, thou deniest thyself, takest up thy daily cross, and followest Him in the Regeneration. This is peremptory, it admits of no reserve or evasion, it is the one way to Christ and eternal life. But be where thou wilt, either here or at Rome, or Geneva, if Self is undenied.

if thou livest to thine own will, to the pleasures of thy natural lust and appetites, senses and passions, and in conformity to the vain customs and spirit of this world, thou art dead whilst thou livest, the seed of the Woman is crucified within thee, Christ can profit thee nothing, thou art a stranger to all that is holy and heavenly within thee, and utterly incapable of finding the peace and joy of God in thy soul. And thus thou art poor, and blind, and naked, and empty, and livest a miserable life in the vanity of time, whilst all the riches of eternity, the light and spirit, the wisdom and love, the peace and joy of God are within thee. And thus it will always be with thee, there is no remedy, go where thou wilt, do what thou wilt, all is shut up, there is no open door of salvation, no awakening out of the sleep of sin, no deliverance from the power of thy corrupt nature, no overcoming of the world no revelation of Jesus Christ, no joy of the new birth from above, till dying to thy self and the world, thou turnest to the light and spirit and power of God in thy soul. All is fruitless and insignificant all the means of thy redemption are at a stand, all outward forms are but a dead formality, till this Fountain of Living Water is found within thee.

But that thou mayest do all this the better, and be more firmly assured that this resignation to and dependence upon the working of God's Spirit within thee is right and sound, I shall lay before thee two great and infallible and fundamental truths, which will be as a rock for thy faith to stand upon. First, that through all the whole nature of things nothing can do, or be a real good to thy soul but the operation of God upon it. Secondly, that all the dispensations of God to mankind from the Fall of Adam to the preaching of the Gospel were only for this one end, to fit, prepare and dispose the soul for the operation of the Spirit of God upon it. These two great truths well and deeply apprehended, put the soul in its right state, in a continual dependence upon God, in a readiness to receive all good from Him, and will be a continual source of light in thy mind. They will keep thee safe from all errors, and false zeal in things and forms of religion, from a sectarian spirit, from bigotry and superstition; they will teach thee the true difference between the means and end of religion, and the regard thou showest to the shell will be only so far as the kernel is to be found in it.

Man, by his fall, had broken off from his true centre, his proper place in God, and therefore the life and operation of God was no more in him. He had fallen from a life in God into a life of self, into an animal life of self-love, self-esteem, and self-seeking in the poor perishing enjoyments of this world. This was the natural state of man by the Fall. He was an apostate from God, and his natural life was all idolatry, where self was the great idol that was worshipped instead of God. See here the whole truth in short. All Sin, Death, Damnation and Hell is nothing else but this Kingdom of Self, or the various operations of self-love, self-esteem and self-seeking, which separate the soul from God and end in eternal Death and Hell.

On the other hand, all that is grace, redemption, salvation, sanctification, spiritual life and the new birth, is nothing else but so much of the life and operation of God found again in the soul. It is man come back again into his centre or place in God, from whence he had broken off. The beginning again of the life of God in the soul was then first made, when the mercy of God inspoke into Adam a seed of the Divine Life, which should bruise the head of the Serpent which had wrought itself into human nature. Here the Kingdom of God was again within us, though only as a seed, yet small as it was, it was yet a degree of the Divine Life which if rightly cultivated would overcome all the evil that was in us, and make of every fallen man a new-born Son of God.

All the sacrifices and institutions of the ancient patri-
archs, the Law of Moses, with all its types and rites and
ceremonies had this only end, they were the methods of
Divine wisdom for a time to keep the hearts of men from
the wanderings of idolatry, in a state of holy expectation
upon God, they were to keep the first seed of life in a state
of growth, and make way for the further operation of God
upon the soul, or, as the Apostle speaks, to be a school-
master unto Christ, that is, till the birth, the Death, the
Resurrection and Ascension of 'Christ should conquer
Death and Hell, open a new Dispensation of God, and
baptize mankind afresh with the Holy Ghost, and Fire of
Heaven. Then, that is, on the Day of Pentecost, a new
Dispensation of God came forth, which on God's part was
the operation of the Holy Spirit in gifts and graces upon
the whole Church, and on man's part, it was the adoration
of God in spirit and in truth. Thus all that was done by
God from the Bruiser of the Serpent given to Adam, to
Christ's sitting down on the right hand of God, was all for
this end, to remove all that stood between God and Man,
and to make way for the immediate and continual operation of God upon the soul, and that man, baptized with the
Holy Spirit and born again from above, should absolutely
renounce Self and wholly give up his soul to the operation
of God's Spirit, to know, to love, to will, to pray, to
worship, to preach, to exhort, to use all the faculties
of his mind, and all the outward things of this world as
enlightened, inspired, moved and guided by the Holy
Ghost, who by this last dispensation of God was given
to be a Comforter, a Teacher and Guide to the Church,
who should abide with it for ever.

This is Christianity, a Spiritual Society, not because it
has no worldly concerns, but because all its members, as
such, are born of the Spirit, kept alive, animated and
governed by the Spirit of God. It is constantly called by our
Lord the Kingdom of God, or Heaven, because all its

ministry and service, all that is done in it, is done in obedience and subjection to that Spirit by which Angels live and are governed in Heaven. Hence our Blessed Lord taught His disciples to pray that this Kingdom might come, that so God's Will might be done on Earth, as it is in Heaven, which could not be but by that same Spirit by which it is done in Heaven. The short is this: The Kingdom of Self is the Fall of Man, or the great apostasy from the life of God in the soul, and everyone wherever he be, that lives unto self is still under the fall and great apostasy from God. The Kingdom of Christ is the spirit and power of God dwelling and manifesting itself in the birth of a new inward man, and no one is a member of this Kingdom, but so far as a true birth of the Spirit is brought forth in him. These two Kingdoms take in all mankind, he that is not of one, is certainly in the other. Dying to one is living to the other.

When therefore the first spark of a desire after God arises in thy soul, cherish it with all thy care, give all thy heart into it, it is nothing less than a touch of the Divine Loadstone that is to draw thee out of the vanity of time into the riches of eternity. Get up therefore and follow it as gladly as the Wise men of the East followed the star from Heaven that appeared to them. It will do for thee as the star did for them, it will lead thee to the birth of Jesus, not in a stable at Bethlehem in Judaea, but to the birth of Jesus in the dark centre of thy own fallen soul.

A PRAYER

Oh heavenly Father, infinite fathomless Depth of never-ceasing Love, save me from myself, from the disorderly workings of my fallen, long corrupted nature, and let my eyes see, my heart and spirit feel and find, thy Salvation in Christ Jesus. O God, who madest me for Thyself to show forth Thy goodness in me, manifest

I humbly beseech Thee, the life-giving power of Thy Holy Nature within me; help me to such a true and living Faith in Thee, such Strength of hunger and thirst after the Birth, Life and Spirit of Thy Holy Jesus in my soul that all that is within me may be turned from every inward thought, or outward work, that is not Thee, Thy Holy Jesus, and heavenly working in my soul. *Amen.*

LOVE IS the great creating Fiat that brought forth every thing, that is distinct from God, and is the only working principle that stirs and effects every thing that is done in Nature and Creature. Love is the principle of generation from the highest to the lowest of creatures. It is the first beginning of every seed of life, every thing that has its form from it, every thing that is born is born in the likeness and with the fruitfulness of that same love that generates and bears it, and this is its own seed of love within itself, and is its power of fructifying its kind.

Love is the holy, heavenly, magic power of the Deity, the first Fiat of God, and all Angels, all eternal beings, are the first births of it. The Deity delights in beholding the ideal images which rise up and appear in the mirror of His own eternal Wisdom. This delight becomes a loving desire to have living creatures in the form of these ideas, and this loving desire is the generating heavenly Parent out of which Angels and all eternal beings are born. Every birth in nature is a consequence of the first prolific love of the Deity, and generates from that which began the first birth. Hence it is that through all the scale of beings, from the top to the bottom of Nature, love is the one principle of generation of every life, and every thing generates from the same principle, and by the same power, by which itself was generated. Marvel not therefore, my Friend, that Adam, standing in the power of his first birth, should have a divine power of bringing forth his own likeness. But I must now tell you that the greatest proof of this glorious truth is yet to come. For I will show you that all the Gospel bears witness to that heavenly birth which we should have had from Adam alone. This birth from Adam is still the one purpose of God, and must be the one way of all those that are to rise with Christ to an equality with the Angels of God. All must be children of Adam, for all that are born of man and woman must lay aside this polluted birth and be born again of a second Adam, in that same perfection of an holy angelic nature which they should have had from the first Adam, before his Eve was separated from him. For it is an undeniable truth of the Gospel that we are called to a new birth, different in its whole nature from that which we have from man and woman, or there is no salvation, and therefore it is certain from the Gospel that the birth which we have from Adam, divided into male and female, is not the birth that we should have had because it is the one reason why we are under a necessity of being born again of a birth from a second Adam, who is to generate us again in that purity and divine power in and by which we should have been born of the first angelic Adam.

A divine love in the first pure and holy Adam, united with the love of God, willing him to be the father of an holy offspring, was to have given birth to a race of creatures from him. But Adam fulfilled not this purpose of God. He awakened in himself a false love, and so all his offspring were forced to be born of man and woman, and thereby to have such impure flesh and blood as cannot enter into the Kingdom of Heaven. Is not this proof enough that this birth from Adam and Eve is not the first birth that we should have had? Will anyone say, How could Adam have such a power to bring from a birth in such a spiritual way, and so contrary to the present state of nature? The whole nature of the Gospel is a full answer to this question. For are we not all to be born again in the same spiritual way, and are we not, merely by a spiritual power, to have a birth of heavenly flesh and blood? The strangeness of such a power in the first Adam is only just so strange and hard to be believed as the same power in the second Adam, who is called the second Adam for no other reason but because He stands in the place of the first, and is to do that which the first should have done. And therefore our having from him a new heavenly flesh and blood raised in us by a spiritual power, superior to the common way of birth in this world, is the strongest of proofs that we should have been born of Adam in the same spiritual power and so contrary to the birth of animals into this world. For all that we have from the second Adam is a proof that we should have had the same from Adam the first—a divine love in Adam the first was to have brought forth an holy offspring. A divine faith now takes its place in the second birth, and is to generate a new birth from the second Adam is to eat His Flesh and drink His Blood, by the same divine power, by which we should have had a birth of the angelic flesh and blood of our first parent.

The continuation of the world though fallen, is a glorious proof and instance of the goodness of God, that so a race of new-born Angels may be brought forth in it. Happy therefore is it that we have such a world as this to be born into, since we are only born to be born again to the life of Heaven. Now Marriage has the nature of this fallen world, but it is God's appointed means of raising the seed of Adam to its full number. Honourable therefore is marriage in our fallen state and happy is it for man to derive his life from it, as it helps him to a power of being eternally a Son of God. Nor does this original of marriage cast the smallest reflection upon the sex, as if they brought all, or any impurity into the human nature. No, by no means. The impurity lies in the division and that which caused it, and not in either of the divided parts. And the female part has this distinction, though not to boast of, yet to take comfort in, that the Saviour of the World is called the Seed of the Woman, and had His birth only from the female part of our divided nature.

Again, if you consider the Fall of Man only as a single act of disobedience to a positive, arbitrary command of God, this is to make all the consequences of his Fall inexplicable. For had the first sin been only a single act of disobedience, it had been more worthy of pardon than any other sin, merely because it was the first, and by a creature that had as yet no experience. But to make the first single act of disobedience not only unpardonable but the cause of such a curse and variety of misery entailed upon all his posterity from the beginning to the end of time, and to suppose that so much wrath was raised in God at this single act of disobedience that nothing could make an Atonement for it but the stupendous mystery of the Birth, Sufferings and Death of the Son of God is yet further impossible to be accounted for. In this case, the supposed wrath and goodness of God are equally inexplicable. And from hence alone have sprung up the detestable doctrines about the guilt and imputation of the first sin, and the several sorts of partial, absolute elections and reprobations of some to eternal happiness, and others to be firebrands of Hell to all eternity. Detestable they may well be called, since if Lucifer could truly say that God from all eternity determined and created him to be that wicked hellish creature that he is, he might then add, Not unto him, but unto his Creator must all his wickedness be ascribed. How innocent, how tolerable is the error of Transubstantiation when compared with this absolute Election and Reprobation! It indeed cannot be reconciled to our senses and reason, but then it leaves God and Heaven possessed of all that is holy and good, but this Reprobation-Doctrine not only overlooks all sense and reason, but confounds Heaven and Hell, takes all goodness from the Deity, and leaves us nothing to detest in the sinner, but God's eternal irresistible contrivance to make him to be such.

We see with open eyes that as a spirit of longing after the life of this world made Adam and us to be the poor pilgrims on earth that we are, so the Spirit of Prayer, or the longing desire of the heart after Christ and God and Heaven breaks all our bonds asunder, casts all our cords from us and raises us out of the miseries of time into the riches of eternity. Thus seeing and knowing our first and present state, everything calls us to prayer, and the desire of the heart becomes the Spirit of Prayer. And when the Spirit of Prayer is born in us, then prayer is no longer considered as only the business of this or that hour, but is the continual panting or breathing of the heart after God. Its petitions are not picked out of manuals of devotion; it loves its own language, it speaks most when it speaks least. If you ask what its words are, they are spirit, they are life, they are love that unite with God.

Choose any life, but the life of God and Heaven, and you choose death, for death is nothing else but the loss of the life of God. The creatures of this world have but one life, and that is the life of this world. This is their one life and one good. Eternal beings have but one life, and one good and that is the life of God. The spirit of the soul is in itself nothing else but a spirit breathed forth from the life of God, and for this only end, that the life of God, the nature of God, the working of God, the tempers of God might be manifested in it. God could not create man to have a will of his own, and a life of his own different from the life and will that is in Himself. This is more impossible than for a good tree to bring forth corrupt fruit. God can only delight in His own life, His own goodness and His own perfection, and therefore cannot love or delight or dwell in any creatures but where His own goodness and perfections are to be found. Like can only unite with like, Heaven with Heaven and Hell with Hell, and therefore the life of God must be the life of the soul if the soul is to unite with God.

Hence it is with all the religion of fallen man, all the methods of our Redemption have only this one end, to take from us that strange and earthly life we have gotten by the Fall, and to kindle again the life of God and Heaven in our souls. Not to deliver us from that gross and sordid vice call coveteousness, which heathens can condemn, but to take the whole spirit of this world entirely from us, and that for this necessary reason because '*All that is in the world, the lust of the flesh, the lust of the eyes and the pride of life is not of the Father*', that is, is not that life, or spirit, of life which we had from God by our creation 'but is of this world', is brought into us by our fall from God into. And therefore a worldly spirit is not to be considered as a single sin or as something that may consist with some real degrees of Christian goodness, but as a state of real death to the kingdom and life of God in our souls. Management, prudence, or an artful trimming betwixt God and Mammon are here all in vain. It is not only the grossness of an outward, visible, worldly behaviour, but the spirit, the prudence, the subtlety, the wisdom of this world that is our separation from the life of God.

The measure of our life is the measure of our knowledge, and as the spirit of our life works, so the spirit of our understanding conceives. If our will works, though our natural capacity be ever so mean and narrow, we get a real knowledge of God and heavenly truths, for everything must feel that in which it lives. But if our will works with Satan, and the spirit of this world, let our parts be ever so bright, our imaginations ever so soaring, yet all our living knowledge, or real sensibility can go no higher or deeper than the mysteries of iniquity and the lusts of flesh and blood. For where our life is, there, and there only is our understanding, and that for this plain reason, because as life is the beginning of all sensibility, so it is and must be the bounds of it, and no sensibility can go any further than the life goes, or have any other manner of knowledge than as the manner of its life is. If you ask what life is, or what is to be understood by it? It is in itself nothing else but a working will, and no life could be either good or evil, but for this reason, because it is a working will.

Every life from the highest angel to the lowest animal consists in a working will and therefore as the will works, as that is with which it unites, so has every creature its degree and kind and manner of life, and consequently, as the will of its life works, so it has its degree and kind and manner of conceiving and understanding, of liking and disliking. For nothing feels or tastes or understands or likes or dislikes but the life that is in us. The spirit that leads our life is the spirit that forms our understanding. The mind is our eye and all the faculties of the mind see everything according to the state the mind is in. If selfish pride is the spirit of our life, everything is only seen, and felt, and known through this glass. Everything is dark, senseless and absurd to the proud man, but that which brings food to this spirit. He understands nothing, he feels nothing, he tastes nothing, but as his pride is made sensible of it, or capable of being affected with it. His working will, which is the life of his soul, lives and works only in the element of pride, and therefore what suits his pride is his only good; and what contradicts his pride is all the evil that he can feel or know. His wit, his parts, his learning, his advancement, his friends, his admirers, his successes, his conquests, all these are the only God and Heaven that he has any living sensibility of. He indeed can talk of a Scripture-God, a Scripture-Christ and Heaven, but these are only the ornamental furniture of his brain, whilst pride is the God of his heart.

We are told that *God resisteth the proud, and giveth grace to the humble*. This is not to be understood as if God, by an arbitrary Will only chose to deal thus with the proud and humble man. Oh no. The true ground is this, the resistance is on the part of man. Pride resisteth God, it rejects Him, it turns from Him and chooses to worship and adore something else instead of Him, whereas Humility leaves all for God, falls down before Him and opens all the doors of the heart for His entrance into it. This is the only sense in which God resisteth the proud and giveth grace to the humble. And thus it is in the true ground and reason of every good and evil that rises up in us. We have neither good nor evil, but as it is the natural effect of the workings of our will, either with or against God, and God only interposes with His threatenings and instructions to direct us to the right use of our wills that we may not blindly work ourselves into death instead of life. But take now another instance like that already mentioned. Look at a man whose working will is under the power of wrath. He sees and hears and feels and understands and talks wholly from the light and sense of wrath. All his faculties are only so many faculties of wrath, and he knows of no sense or reason but that which his enlightened wrath discovers to him.

I have appealed to these instances only to illustrate and confirm that great truth, which I before asserted, namely, that the working of our will, or the state of our life, governs the state of our mind, and forms the degree and manner of our understanding and knowledge, and that as the fire of our life burns, so is the light of our life kindled. And all this only to show you the utter impossibility of knowing God and divine truths till your life is divine, and wholly dead to the life and spirit of this world, since our light and knowledge can be no better or higher than the state of our life and heart is.

The Spirit of Prayer is a pressing forth of the soul out of this earthly life. It is a stretching with all its desire after the life of God. It is a leaving, as far as it can, all its own spirit to receive a Spirit from above, to be one life, one love, one spirit with Christ in God. This prayer, which is an emptying itself of all its own lusts and natural tempers, and an opening itself for the light and love of God to enter into it, is the prayer in the Name of Christ, to which nothing is denied. For the love which God bears to the soul, His eternal, never-ceasing desire to enter into it, to dwell in it, and open the birth of His Holy Word and Spirit in it stays no longer than till the door of the heart opens for Him. For nothing does, or can keep God out of the soul, or hinder His holy union with it, but the desire of the heart turned from Him. And the reason of it is this. It is because the life of the soul is in itself nothing else but a working will and therefore wherever the will works or goes, there, and there only, the soul lives, whether it be in God or the creature.

Nothing does or can go with a man into Heaven. Nothing follows him into Hell, but that in which the will dwelt, with which it was fed, nourished and clothed in this life. And this is to be noted well, that death can make no alteration of this state of the will. It only takes off the outward, worldly covering of flesh and blood, and forces the soul to see and feel and know what a life, what a state, food, body and habitation, its own working will has brought forth in it.

Tell me, is there anything in life that deserves a thought, but how to keep this working of our will in a right state, and to get that purity of heart which alone can see and know and find and possess God? Is there anything so frightful as this worldly spirit which turns the soul from God, makes it an House of Darkness, and feeds it with the food of time at the expense of all the riches of eternity? On the other hand, what can be so desirable a good as the Spirit of Prayer, which empties the soul of all its own evil, separates death and darkness from it, leaves Self, time and the world, and becomes one life, one light, one love, one spirit with Christ and God and Heaven?

Think, my Friends, of these things with something more than thoughts. Let your hungry souls eat of the nourishment of them as a bread of Heaven, and desire only to live that with all the working of your wills and the whole spirit of your minds, you may live and die united to God.

There is no true and real Conversion, whether it be from infidelity, or any other life of sin, till a man comes to know and feel that nothing less than his whole nature is to be parted with, and yet finds in himself no possibility of doing it. This is the inability that can bring us at last to say with the Apostle, *When I am weak, then am I strong.* This is the distress that stands near to the Gate of Life. This is the despair by which we lose all our own life, to find a new one in God. For here, in this place it is, that faith and hope and true seeking to God and Christ are born. But till all is despair in ourselves, till all is lost that we had any trust in as our own, till then, faith and hope and turning to God in prayer, are only things learnt and practised by rule and method, but they are not born in us, are not living qualities of a new birth, till we have done feeling any trust or confidence in ourselves.

All religion is the Spirit of Love. All its gifts and graces are the gifts and graces of Love. It has no breath, no life, but the life of Love. Nothing exalts, nothing purifies, but the fire of Love. Nothing changes Death into life, Earth into Heaven, Men into Angels, but Love alone. Loves breathes the spirit of God: its words and works are the inspiration of God. It speaketh not of itself, but the Word, the eternal Word of God speaketh in it. For all that Love speaketh, that God speaketh, because Love is God. Love is Heaven revealed in the soul. It is light and truth. It is infallible. It has no errors, for all errors are the want of Love. Love has no more of pride than light has of darkness. It stands and bears all its fruits from a depth and root of Humility. Love is of no sect or party. It neither makes nor admits of any bounds. You may as easily inclose the light, or shut up the air of the world into one place as confine Love to a sect or party. It lives in the liberty, the universality, the impartiality of Heaven. It believes in One, Holy, Catholic God, the God of all spirits. It unites and joins with all that is good and is meek, patient, well-wishing and long-

suffering over all the evil that is in nature and creature. Love,
like the Spirit of God, rideth upon the wings of the wind,
and is in union and communion with all the saints that are
in Heaven and on earth. Love is quite pure. It has no by-
ends. It seeks not its own. It has but one will, and that is to
give itself into everything, and overcome all evil with good.

Lastly, Love is the Christ of God. It comes down from
Heaven. It regenerates the soul from above. It blots out
all transgressions. It takes from death its sting, from the
Devil his power, and from the Serpent his poison. It heals
all infirmities of our earthly birth. It gives eyes to the blind,
ears to the deaf, and makes the dumb to speak. It cleanses
the lepers, and casts out Devils, and puts man in Paradise
before he dies.

Here, therefore, we are come to this firm conclusion,
that let religion have ever so many shapes, forms or refor-
mations, it is no true divine service, no proper worship
of God, has no good in it, can do no good to man, can
remove no evil out of him, raise no divine life in him, but
so far as it serves, worships, conforms and gives itself up
to this operation of the Holy Triune God, as living and
dwelling in the soul. Keep close to the idea of religion,
as an inward spiritual life of the soul. Observe all its works
within you, the death and life that are found there. Seek
for no good, no comfort, but in the inward awakening of
all that is holy and heavenly in your heart, and then so
much as you have of this inward religion, so much you have
of a real salvation.

For salvation is only a victory over Nature. So far as you
resist and renounce your own vain, selfish and earthly
nature, so far as you overcome all your own natural
tempers of the old Man, so far God enters into you, lives
and operates in you, He is in you the light, the life and the
spirit of your soul, and you are in Him the new creature
that worships Him in spirit and in truth. For divine worship or service is, and can only be performed, by being

like minded with Christ. Nothing worships God, but the Spirit of Christ His Beloved Son, in whom He is well pleased. This is as true as that *no man hath known the Father, but the Son, and He to whom the Son revealed Him.*

Look now at anything as religion, or divine service, but a strict, unerring conformity to the life and spirit of Christ, and then though every day were full of burnt offerings, and sacrifices, yet you would be only like those religionists who *drew near to God with their lips, but their hearts were far from Him.* For the heart is always far from God, unless the spirit of Christ be alive in it.

People may be daily at the Service of the Church and read long prayers at home, in which are many petitions for the Holy Spirit, and yet live and die, led and governed by the spirit of the world, because all these prayers, whether we hear them read by others, or read them ourselves, may be done in compliance only to duties, rules and forms of religion, as things we are taught not to neglect, but being only done thus, they are not the true, real working of the spirit of the heart, nor make any real alteration in it.

Every spirit necessarily reaps that which it sows. It cannot possibly be otherwise. It is the unalterable procedure of Nature. Everything proceeds from it, is born from it, yields to it, and is governed by it. If the spirit soweth to the flesh, it reapeth that corruption which belongs to the flesh. If it soweth to the spirit, it reapeth the fruits of the Spirit, which are eternal life. The Spirit of Prayer, therefore, is the opener of all that is good within us, and the receiver of all that is good without us. It unites with God, is one power in Him. It works with Him, and drives all that is not God out of the soul. The soul is no longer a slave to its natural impurity and corruption, no longer imprisoned in its own death and darkness, but till the fire from Heaven, the Spirit of Prayer is kindled in it. Then begins the Resurrection and the Life, and all that which died in Adam comes to life in Christ.

This is the true nature of the spiritual life, it is as truly a growth or vegetation as that of plants, and nothing but its own hunger can help it to the true food of its life. If this hunger of the soul ceases, it withers and dies, though in the midst of divine plenty. Our Lord, to show us that the new birth is really a state of spiritual vegetation, compares it to a small grain of mustard-seed from whence a great plant arises. Now every seed has a life in itself, or else it could not grow.

What is this life?

It is nothing else but an hunger of the seed after the air and light of this world, which hunger, being met and fed by the light and air of Nature, changes the seed into a living plant. Thus it is with the Seed of Heaven in the soul. It has a life in itself, or else no life could arise from it.

What is this life?

It is nothing else but faith, or an hunger after God and Heaven, which no sooner stirs, or is suffered to stir, but it is met, embraced and quickened by the light and spirit of God and Heaven, and so a new man in Christ is formed from the Seed of Heaven, as a new plant from a seed in the earth. Let us suppose now that the seed of a plant had sense and reason, and that instead of continually hungering after and drawing in the virtue of the light and air of our outward nature, it should amuse and content its hunger with reasoning about the nature of hunger, and the different powers and virtues of light and air, must not such a seed of all necessity wither away, without ever becoming a living plant?

Now this is no false similitude of the seed of life in man. Man has a power of drawing all the virtue of Heaven into himself, because the seed of heaven is the gift of God in his soul, which wants the light and spirit of God to bring it to the birth, just as the seed of the plant wants the light and air of this world. It cannot possibly grow up in God but by taking in light, life and spirit from Heaven, as the creatures of time take in the light and life and spirit of this world. If therefore the soul, instead of hungering after Heaven, instead of eating the Flesh and Blood of the Christ of God contents and amuses this Seed of Life with ideas and notions and sounds must not such a soul of necessity wither and die, without ever becoming a living creature of Heaven? Wonder not therefore that all the work of our Salvation and Regeneration is, by the Scripture, wholly confined to the operation of the light and spirit of God living and working in us.

Thus you see that God is all; that nothing but His life and working power in us can be our Salvation, and yet that nothing but the Spirit of Prayer can make it possible for us to have it, or be capable of it. And therefore neither you, nor any other human soul, can be without the operation of the light and spirit of God in it, but because its will-spirit, or its Spirit of Prayer, is turned towards something else, for we are always in union with that with which our will is united.

I say, praying for something else, for you are to notice this, as a certain truth that every man's life is a continual state of prayer. He is no moment free from it, nor can possibly be so. For all our natural tempers, be they what they will, ambition, covetousness, selfishness, worldly-mindedness, pride, envy, hatred, malice, or any other lust whatever, are all of them in reality only so many different kinds and forms of a Spirit of Prayer which is as inseparable from the heart as weight is from the body. For every natural temper is nothing else but a manifestation of the desire and prayer of the heart, and shows us how it works and wills. And as the heart worketh and willeth such, and no other, is its prayer. All else is only form and fiction, and empty beating of the air. If therefore the working desire of the heart is not habitually turned towards God, if this is not our Spirit of Prayer, we are necessarily in a state of prayer towards something else that carries us from God, and brings all kind of evil into us.

For this is the necessity of our nature, pray we must, as sure as our heart is alive, and therefore when the state of the heart is not a Spirit of Prayer to God, we pray without ceasing to some or other part of the Creation. The man whose heart habitually tends towards the riches, honours, powers or pleasures of this life, is in a continual state of prayer towards all these things. His spirit stands always bent towards them. They have his hope, his love, his faith, and are the many gods that he worships. And though when he is upon his knees, and uses forms of prayer, he directs them to the God of Heaven, yet these are in reality the God of his heart, and in a sad sense of the words, he really worships them in spirit and in truth. Hence you may see how it comes to pass that there is so much praying and yet so little of true piety amongst us. The bells are daily calling us to Church, our closets abound with manuals of devotion, yet how little fruit! It is all for this reason, because our prayers are not our own. They are not the abundance of our own heart, are not found and felt within us, as we feel our own hunger and thirst, but are only so many borrowed forms of speech which we use at certain times and occasions. And therefore it is no wonder that little good comes of it. What benefit could it have been to the Pharisee if with an heart inwardly full of its own pride and self-exaltation he had outwardly hung down his head, smote upon his breast, and borrowed the publican's words *God be merciful to me a sinner*? What greater good can be expected from our praying in the words of David, or singing his Psalms seven times a day, if our heart has no more of the spirit of David in it than the heart of the Pharisee had of the spirit of the humble Publican?

It is also good for you to think that many of the prayers of the Church may go faster and higher than your heart can in truth go along with them. For this will put you upon a right care over yourself, and so to live that, as a true son to your mother the Church, your heart may be able to speak her language, conform to her service, and find the delight of your soul in the spirit of her prayers. But this will only then come to pass when the Spirit of Prayer is the spirit of your heart. Then, every good word, whether in a form, or out of a form, whether heard or read or thought, will be as suitable to your heart, as gratifying to it as food is to the hungry and drink to the thirsty soul. But till the spirit of the heart is thus renewed, till it is emptied of all earthly desires and stands in an habitual hunger and thirst after God (which is the true Spirit of Prayer) till then all our forms of prayer will be more or less but too much like lessons that are given to scholars, and we shall mostly say them only because we dare not neglect them.

But be not discouraged. Take the following advice, and then you may go to Church without any danger of a mere lip-labour or hypocrisy, although there should be a hymn or a psalm or a prayer whose language is higher than that of your own heart. Do this: Go to the Church as the Publican went to the Temple. Stand inwardly in the spirit of your mind, in that form which he outwardly expressed when he cast down his eyes, smote upon his breast and could only say *God be merciful to me a sinner*. Stand unchangeably (at least in your desire) in this form and state of heart. It will sanctify every petition that comes out of your mouth, and when anything is read, or sung, or prayed, that is more exalted and fervent than your heart is, if you make this an occasion of a further sinking down in the spirit of the publican, you will then be helped, and highly blessed by those prayers and praises which seem only to fit and belong to, a better heart than yours.

This, my Friend, is a Secret of Secrets. It will help you to reap where you have not sown, and be a continual source of grace in your soul. This will not only help you to receive good from those prayers which seem too good for the state of your heart, but will help you to find good from everything else. For everything that inwardly stirs you,

THE POCKET WILLIAM LAW

or outwardly happens to you becomes a real good to you, if it either finds or excites in you this humble form of mind. For nothing is in vain, or without profit to the humble soul. Like the bee, it takes its honey even from bitter herbs. It stands always in a state of divine growth, and everything that falls upon it is like a dew of Heaven to it.

Shut up yourself therefore in this form of humility, all good is enclosed in it. It is a water of Heaven that turns the fire of the fallen soul into the meekness of the divine life, and creates that oil out of which the love of God and man gets its flame. Be inclosed therefore always in it. Let it be as a garment wherewith you are always covered, and the girdle with which you are girt. Breathe nothing but in and from its spirit. See nothing but with its eyes. Hear nothing, but with its ears. And then, whether you are in the Church, or out of the Church, hearing the praises of God, or receiving wrongs from men and the world, all will be edification and every thing will help forward your growth in the life of God.

The painful sense and feeling of what you are, kindled into a state of sensibility by the light of God within you, is the fire and light from whence your Spirit of Prayer proceeds. In its first kindling nothing is found or felt but pain, wrath and darkness, as is to be seen in the first kindling of every heat or fire. And therefore its first prayer is nothing else but a sense of penitence, self-condemnation, confession and humility. This Prayer of Humility is met by the divine love, the mercifulness of God embraces it, and then its prayer is changed into hymns and songs and thanksgivings. When this state of fervour has done its work, has melted away all earthly passions and affections, and left no inclination in the soul but to delight in God alone, then its prayer changes again. It is now come so near to God, has found such union with Him, that it does not so much pray as live in God. Its prayer is not any particular action, is not the work of any particular faculty, not confined to times, words, or place but is the work of his whole being which continually stands in fulness of faith, in purity of love, in absolute resignation to do and be what and how his Beloved pleases. This is the last state of the Spirit of Prayer and is its highest union with God in this life.

People who have long dwelt in the fervours of devotion, in an high sensibility of divine affections, practising every virtue, with a kind of greediness, are frightened when coldness seizes upon them, when their hymns give no transport, and their hearts, instead of flaming with the love of every virtue, seem ready to be overcome by every vice. But here keep fast hold of the thread I mentioned before, and all is well. For this coldness is the divine offspring or genuine birth of the former fervour. It comes from it as a good fruit and brings the soul nearer to God than the fervour did. The fervour was good, and did a good work in the soul. It overcame the earthly nature and made the soul delight in God and spiritual things, but its delight was too much an own delight, a fancied self-holiness and occasioned rest and satisfaction in self which if it had continued unin-terrupted, undiscovered, an earthly self had only been changed into a spiritual self. Therefore I called this cold-ness or loss of fervour its divine offspring, because it brings a divine effect, or more fruitful progress in the divine life. For this coldness overcomes and delivers us from spiritual self, as fervour overcame the earthly nature. It does the work that fervour did, but in an higher degree, because it gives up more, sacrifices more, and brings forth more resignation to God than fervour did, and therefore it is more in God and receives more from Him. The devout soul therefore is always safe in every state if it makes everything an occasion of either rising up, or falling down into the hands of God, and exercising faith, and trust, and resignation to Him.

Fervour is good and ought to be loved, but tribulation, distress and coldness in their season are better, because they give means and power of exercising faith, a purer love, and more perfect resignation to God which are the best state of the soul. And therefore the pious soul that eyes only God, that means nothing but being His alone, can have no stop to its progress; light and darkness equally assist him. In the light he looks up to God. In the darkness he lays hold on God, and so they both do him the same good.

The way to be a man of prayer and be governed by its spirit is not to get a book full of prayers, but the best help you can have from a book is to read one full of such truths, instructions and awakening informations as force you to see and know who, and what, and where you are; that God is your All; and that all is misery but a heart and life devoted to Him. This is the best outward Prayer Book you can have, as it will turn you to an inward book, and Spirit of Prayer in your heart, which is a continual, longing desire of the heart after God, his Divine Life and Holy Spirit. When, for the sake of this inward prayer you retire at any time of the day never begin till you know and feel why and wherefore you are going to pray; and let this why and wherefore form and direct everything that comes from you, whether it be in thought or word. As you cannot but know your own state, so it must be the easiest thing in the world to look up to God with such desires as suit the state you are in, and praying in this manner, whether it be in one, or more, or no words, your prayer will always be sincere, and good, and highly beneficial to you. Thus praying, you can never pray in vain, but one month in the practice of it will do you more good, make a greater change in your soul, than twenty years of prayer only by books, and forms of other people's making.

The Holy Spirit of God is as necessary to our divine life or the life of grace, as the air of this world is necessary to our animal life, and is as distinct from us, and as much without us, as the air of this world is distinct from, and without the creatures that live in it. And yet our own good spirit is the very Spirit of God, moving and stirring in us. No animal can unite with, or breathe the air of this world till it has first the air of this world brought forth, as the true birth of its own life in itself. This is its only capacity to live in the spirit of this world, and the breath or spirit that thus arises is its own life, is the very same breath, that is in outward nature, in which it lives. It is strictly thus with the Spirit of God in our souls. It must first have a birth within us, arising from the life of our souls, and as such, is our only capacity to have life, and live in the Spirit of God Himself, and is the very breath of the Spirit of God, who is yet as distinct from us as the breath of our animal life that arises from our own fire is distinct from the air of the world in which it lives. And thus our own good spirit is the very Spirit of the Deity, and yet not God, but the Spirit of God breathed or kindled into a creaturely form, and this good spirit, divine in its origin, and divine in its nature, is that alone in us that can reach God, unite with Him, co-operate with Him, be moved and blessed by Him, as our earthly spirit is by the outward spirit of the elementary world.

Would you know what it is to love God with all your heart and soul, you need only look back to that which has been said of the nature and spirit of God. For when with all your heart and soul you love and long to have that nature and spirit, to be wholly united to it, possessed and governed by it, then you love God with all your heart and soul. And then you are first capable of loving yourself and your neighbour rightly. For so much as you have of the Divine Nature and Spirit in you, just so much power have you of loving yourself and your neighbour aright; that is of loving only and equally that in yourself and your neighbour which the Deity only and equally loves, both in you and Him.